Learning Python Testing

A straightforward and easy approach to testing your Python projects

Daniel Arbuckle

[PACKT] PUBLISHING
open source
community experience distilled

BIRMINGHAM - MUMBAI

Learning Python Testing

First published: January 2010

Second edition: November 2014

Production reference: 1181114

Published by Packt Publishing Ltd.
Livery Place
35 Livery Street
Birmingham B3 2PB, UK.

ISBN 978-1-78355-321-1

www.packtpub.com

Cover image by Prasanna BC (prasannabc@gmail.com)

Credits

Author
Daniel Arbuckle

Reviewers
Tarun Behal
Johnson M. R. Chetty
Brian Escribano
Piyush Gururani
Marko Klemetti
Sean Robinson
Michael Tsai

Acquisition Editor
Owen Roberts

Content Development Editor
Arvind Koul

Technical Editor
Venu Manthena

Copy Editor
Rashmi Sawant

Project Coordinator
Priyanka Goel

Proofreaders
Stephen Copestake
Ameesha Green

Indexer
Monica Ajmera Mehta

Graphics
Sheetal Aute
Valentina D'silva

Production Coordinator
Nilesh R. Mohite

Cover Work
Nilesh R. Mohite

About the Author

Daniel Arbuckle received his PhD. degree in Computer Science from the University of Southern California in 2007. He is an active member of the Python community and an avid unit tester.

I would like to thank Grig, Titus, and my family for their companionship and encouragement along the way.

About the Reviewers

Tarun Behal is a fervent software developer currently living in Delhi, India. After starting his career in the field of IT, where he worked as an ERP consultant, he's now a web application developer with interests ranging from architecture to designing web applications delivering great user experience. He's passionate about open source technologies and web applications, and contributes to communities.

Tarun went to Uttar Pradesh Technical University (India) and graduated with a Bachelor of Technology degree in Information Technology. He now works for Nagarro Software Pvt. Ltd, a leading service-based IT company.

The quickest way to reach him is via LinkedIn at `https://www.linkedin.com/in/tarunbehal`.

I feel much honored to have been asked to review this book. This was an amazing experience for me, as I learned a lot at the same time, and I am sure you will too.

I'd like to thank my family specially my brother, Varun, and my colleagues Shipra, Denis, Prabhansh, Prafful, Shubham, Arun, Mansi, and Rachita for their constant support and motivation. Also, I would like to thank all the members of the Python community.

Johnson M. R. Chetty is an avid open data proponent. He works primarily with Python, JavaScript, and Linux to enable end-to-end solutions.

Working with real-world data to meet objectives is something that he finds challenging and likes to grapple with. His primary focus is on areas such as data visualization, data analysis, Semantic Web, GIS, systems deployment and scaling (Linux), mentoring, and project management. He has worked with Gnowledge Lab (Homi Bhabha Centre for Science Education, TIFR), GISE Lab (IIT Bombay), NCERT, ChaloBEST, CAMP, ZLemma, and Wishtel among others.

He was a mentor for Google Summer of Code 2012 for the GNOWSYS platform—a GNU/Linux project.

He is interested in technology, scientific data, economics, and looking at the world to know where it's currently headed. You will also find him keenly following advances in Brain Science, AI, GIS, Semantic Web, and Internet of Things.

He likes to think of himself as a budding musician and a novice economist.

For more information on his work, kindly visit `http://johnc.in`. You can also find his LinkedIn profile at `http://johnc.in/linkedin` and Google Plus profile at `http://johnc.in/gplus`.

Jesus, Mr. Michael Susai Chetty, and Mrs. Regina Mary deserve a round of applause for managing to put up with a son like me and for giving me all the love and freedom in the world. I would like to thank them for giving me everything I have.

Brian Escribano has over 11 years' experience working in the fields of education, TV, and games. He builds world-class character rigs and animation pipelines for companies such as Nickelodeon, Mirada, Spark Unlimited, and BioWare. With his deep scripting knowledge in Python and MEL, Brian brings a wealth of expertise and experience to any team he works with.

Piyush Gururani is a programmer and core developer working in Mumbai, India. His work has revolved around making applications for large touch screens in Qt, developing a closed source SDK to allow third-party developers to make applications for large touch screens, and designing backend architecture for content and real-time notification delivery in Python and Node.js. He has worked as a senior developer and consultant to start-ups in India and UK.

I would like to acknowledge my mother and father for their efforts in my upbringing and education.

Marko Klemetti (`@mrako`) is a father, leader, and developer. He is currently the head of the leading Finnish Devops unit in Eficode (`http://www.eficode.com`). With his team, he changes the way Finnish and multinational organizations create and purchase software. He is also the founder and architect of Trail (`http://www.entertrail.com`), an internationally successful solution for social asset management.

Marko has specialized in bringing efficiency to large software production environments by applying modern software development practices and tools, such as Continuous Delivery (CD) and Acceptance Test-Driven Development (ATDD). With his two decades of software development experience, he is able to engage both executives and developers in process change. Marko is passionate about making programming both fun and productive at the same time.

Sean Robinson is an award-winning graduate from the University of South Wales, who originally trained as a game developer using C and C++. He was headhunted out of the university to run the development arm of LexAble, a company making assistive technology to help those with dyslexia.

As a lead engineer in the start-up, Sean embarked on an ambitious training regime, teaching himself Mac development, software testing, leadership, coaching, mentoring, and project management in order to best serve the company. Sean has also been responsible for establishing many company policies, including testing, security, code quality, a developer hiring procedure, project management, version control, and ticket management.

Looking for a new challenge, Sean has recently joined a new team and is refocussing his energies on web development.

Sean is a polyglot developer, completely agnostic regarding technology and supremely passionate about learning and personal development. He spends his time volunteering as a STEM Ambassador for Wales, Thai boxing, and scuba diving. You can find him blogging at `www.SeanTRobinson.co.uk` or tweeting at `@SeanTRobinson`.

Michael Tsai went to the Academy of Art University at San Francisco to study Visual Effects. After college, he worked on *Fantastic Four: Rise of the Silver Surfer*, *Red Cliff II*, and the stereoscopic version of *G-Force*. In 2012, Michael received his Master of Entertainment Technology degree (MET) from the Entertainment Technology Center of Carnegie Mellon University. *Elysium* was another feature film he worked on before he joined Schell Games in Pittsburgh as a game/technical artist.

www.PacktPub.com

Support files, eBooks, discount offers, and more

For support files and downloads related to your book, please visit `www.PacktPub.com`.

Did you know that Packt offers eBook versions of every book published, with PDF and ePub files available? You can upgrade to the eBook version at `www.PacktPub.com` and as a print book customer, you are entitled to a discount on the eBook copy. Get in touch with us at `service@packtpub.com` for more details.

At `www.PacktPub.com`, you can also read a collection of free technical articles, sign up for a range of free newsletters and receive exclusive discounts and offers on Packt books and eBooks.

PACKTLIB™

`https://www.packtpub.com/books/subscription/packtlib`

Do you need instant solutions to your IT questions? PacktLib is Packt's online digital book library. Here, you can search, access, and read Packt's entire library of books.

Why subscribe?

- Fully searchable across every book published by Packt
- Copy and paste, print, and bookmark content
- On demand and accessible via a web browser

Free access for Packt account holders

If you have an account with Packt at `www.PacktPub.com`, you can use this to access PacktLib today and view 9 entirely free books. Simply use your login credentials for immediate access.

Table of Contents

Preface

In this book, you'll learn about the major tools, techniques, and skills of automated testing in the Python 3 language. You'll learn about the tools that are included in Python's standard library, such as doctest, unittest, and unittest.mock. You'll also learn about useful nonstandard tools such as Nose and coverage.py. As we're talking about these tools, we'll also be discussing the philosophy and best practices of testing, so when you're done you'll be ready to use what you've learned in real-world projects.

This book is a successor to an earlier book, *Python Testing: Beginner's Guide, Daniel Arbuckle, Packt Publishing* which only covered Python up to version 2.6. Python 3 and its related tools are just slightly too different to justify calling this book a second edition. If you've read the earlier book and parts of this book seem familiar to you, it's because the two books are in fact similar.

What this book covers

Chapter 1, Python and Testing, provides an introduction to formalized and automated testing in Python.

Chapter 2, Working with doctest, teaches you to use doctest, a tool that integrates testing and documentation.

Chapter 3, Unit Testing with doctest, helps you understand how to apply doctest to the discipline of unit testing.

Chapter 4, Decoupling Units with unittest.mock, teaches you to create and use mock objects.

Chapter 5, Structured Testing with unittest, helps you to build more structured test suites with unittest.

Chapter 6, Running Your Tests with Nose, helps you run your doctests, unittests, and more with one command.

Chapter 7, Test-driven Development Walk-through, takes you step by step through the test-driven development process.

Chapter 8, Integration and System Testing, teaches you how to test the interactions between units of code.

Chapter 9, Other Tools and Techniques, helps you learn about continuous integration, version control hooks, and other useful things that are related to testing.

What you need for this book

You're going to need Python version 3.4 or later, a text editor, and Internet access to get the most out of this book.

Who this book is for

This book is primarily for people who have a solid grasp of the Python language, and want a boost in working with automated testing. If you do not know Python at all, this book will still serve as an introduction to automated testing philosophy and practices. Thanks to Python's executable pseudocode nature, though, you might find the road a little bumpy at times.

Conventions

In this book, you will find a number of styles of text that distinguish between different kinds of information. Here are some examples of these styles, and an explanation of their meaning.

Code words in text, database table names, folder names, filenames, file extensions, pathnames, dummy URLs, user input, and Twitter handles are shown as follows: "Mock objects are provided by the `unittest.mock` module in the standard library."

A block of code is set as follows:

```
class ClassOne:
    def __init__(self, arg1, arg2):
        self.arg1 = int(arg1)
        self.arg2 = arg2

    def method1(self, x):
        return x * self.arg1
```

When we wish to draw your attention to a particular part of a code block, the relevant lines or items are set in bold:

```
class ClassOne:
    def __init__(self, arg1, arg2):
        self.arg1 = int(arg1)
        self.arg2 = arg2

    def method1(self, x):
        return x * self.arg1
```

Any command-line input or output is written as follows:

```
$ python -m nose
```

New terms and **important words** are shown in bold.

[Warnings or important notes appear in a box like this.]

[Tips and tricks appear like this.]

Reader feedback

Feedback from our readers is always welcome. Let us know what you think about this book—what you liked or may have disliked. Reader feedback is important for us to develop titles that you really get the most out of.

To send us general feedback, simply send an e-mail to `feedback@packtpub.com`, and mention the book title via the subject of your message.

If there is a topic that you have expertise in and you are interested in either writing or contributing to a book, see our author guide on `www.packtpub.com/authors`.

Customer support

Now that you are the proud owner of a Packt book, we have a number of things to help you to get the most from your purchase.

Downloading the example code

You can download the example code files for all Packt books you have purchased from your account at `http://www.packtpub.com`. If you purchased this book elsewhere, you can visit `http://www.packtpub.com/support` and register to have the files e-mailed directly to you.

Errata

Although we have taken every care to ensure the accuracy of our content, mistakes do happen. If you find a mistake in one of our books—maybe a mistake in the text or the code—we would be grateful if you could report this to us. By doing so, you can save other readers from frustration and help us improve subsequent versions of this book. If you find any errata, please report them by visiting `http://www.packtpub.com/submit-errata`, selecting your book, clicking on the **Errata Submission Form** link, and entering the details of your errata. Once your errata are verified, your submission will be accepted and the errata will be uploaded to our website or added to any list of existing errata under the Errata section of that title.

To view the previously submitted errata, go to `https://www.packtpub.com/books/content/support` and enter the name of the book in the search field. The required information will appear under the **Errata** section.

Piracy

Piracy of copyright material on the Internet is an ongoing problem across all media. At Packt, we take the protection of our copyright and licenses very seriously. If you come across any illegal copies of our works, in any form, on the Internet, please provide us with the location address or website name immediately so that we can pursue a remedy.

Please contact us at `copyright@packtpub.com` with a link to the suspected pirated material.

We appreciate your help in protecting our authors, and our ability to bring you valuable content.

Questions

You can contact us at `questions@packtpub.com` if you are having a problem with any aspect of the book, and we will do our best to address it.

1
Python and Testing

You might be a programmer, a coder, a developer, or maybe a hacker. As such, it's almost impossible that you haven't had to sit down with a program that you were sure was ready for use—or possibly a program you knew was not ready—and put together a bunch of tests to prove it. It often feels like an exercise in futility or, at its best, a waste of time. We're going to learn about how to avoid this situation, and make testing an easy and enjoyable process.

This book is going to show you a new way to test, a way that puts much of the burden of testing right where it should be—on the computer. Even better, your tests will help you to find problems early, and tell you just where they are, so that you can fix them easily. You'll love the easy, helpful methods of automated testing, and test-driven development.

The Python language has some of the best tools when it comes to testing, so we're going to learn about how to make testing easy, quick, fun, and productive by taking advantage of these tools.

This chapter provides an overview of the book, so we're going to briefly discuss the following topics:

- The levels of tests: Unit, integration, and system
- Acceptance testing and regression testing
- Test-driven development

Testing for fun and profit

This chapter started with a lot of grandiose claims—you'll enjoy testing. You'll rely on this to help you kill bugs early and easily. Testing will stop being a burden for you and will become something that you want to do. *How?*

Think back to the last really annoying bug that you had to deal with. It could have been anything: a database schema mismatch, a bad data structure, what have you.

Remember what caused the bug? The one line of code with the subtle logic error. The function that didn't do what the docs said it did. Whatever it was, keep this in mind.

Imagine a small chunk of code that could have caught that bug, if it had been run at the right time and you had been told about it.

Now imagine that all of your code is accompanied by those little chunks of test code, and that they are quick and easy to execute.

How long would your bug have survived? Not very long at all.

This gives you a pretty basic understanding of what we'll be talking about in this book. There are many refinements and tools to make the process quicker and easier, but the basic idea is to tell the computer what you expect, using simple and easily-written chunks of code, and then tell the computer to double-check your expectations throughout the coding process. Because expectations are easy to describe, you can write them down *first*, allowing the computer to shoulder much of the burden of debugging your code. Because expectations are easy to describe, you can write them down *fast*, allowing you to move on to interesting things while the computer keeps track of the rest.

When you're done, you have a code base that is highly tested and that you can be highly confident of. You caught your bugs early and fixed them quickly. Best of all, your testing was done by the computer based on what you told it and what you wanted the program to do. After all, why should you do it, when the computer can do it for you?

I have had simple automated tests catch everything from minor typos to instances of database access code being left dangerously out-of-date after a schema change, and pretty much any other bug that you can imagine. The tests caught the errors quickly and pinpointed their locations. A great deal of effort and trouble was avoided because they were there.

Spending less time on debugging and being sure of your result makes programming more fun. Producing a higher quality of code in a shorter amount of time makes it more profitable. The test suite provides instant feedback, allowing you to run each chunk of your code *now* instead of waiting for the program as a whole to be in a state where you can execute it. This quick turnaround makes programming both more satisfying and more productive.

Levels of testing

Testing is commonly divided into several categories based on how complex the component being tested is. Most of our time will be focused on the lowest level—unit testing—because unit tests provide the foundation for tests in the other categories. Tests in the other categories operate on the same principles.

Unit testing

Unit testing is testing the smallest possible pieces of a program. Often, this means individual functions or methods. The keyword here is individual: something is a "unit" if there's no meaningful way to divide it up further.

For example, it would make sense in order to consider this function as a unit:

```
def quadratic(a, b, c, x):
    return a * (x ** 2) + b * x + c
```

The preceding function works as a unit because breaking it up into smaller pieces is not something that can be practically or usefully done.

Unit tests test a single unit in isolation, verifying that it works as expected without considering what the rest of the program might do. This protects each unit from inheriting bugs from the mistakes made elsewhere, and makes it easy to narrow down where the real problems are.

By itself, unit testing isn't enough to confirm that a complete program works correctly, but it's the foundation on which everything else is based. You can't build a house without solid materials, and you can't build a program without units that work as expected.

Integration testing

In integration testing, the boundaries of isolation are pushed further back, so that the tests encompass the interactions between related units. Each test should still be run in isolation in order to avoid inheriting problems from outside, but now the test checks whether the tested units behave correctly as a group.

Integration testing can be performed with the same tools as unit testing. For this reason, newcomers to automated testing are sometimes lured into ignoring the distinction between unit testing and integration testing. Ignoring this distinction is dangerous because such multipurpose tests often make assumptions about the correctness of some of the units they involve; this means that the tester loses much of the benefit that automated testing would have granted. We're not aware of the assumptions we make until they bite us, so we need to consciously choose to work in a way that minimizes assumptions. That's one of the reasons why I refer to test-driven development as a "discipline."

System testing

System testing extends the boundaries of isolation even further to the point where they don't even exist. System tests check parts of the program after the whole thing has been plugged together. In a sense, system tests are an extreme form of the integration tests.

System tests are very important, but they're not very useful without the integration tests and unit tests backing them up. You have to be sure of the pieces before you can be sure of the whole. If there's a subtle error somewhere, system testing will tell you that it exists, but not where it is or how to fix it. The odds are good that you've experienced this situation before; it's probably why you hate testing. With a properly put together test suite, system tests are almost a formality. Most of the problems are caught by unit tests or integration tests, while the system tests simply provide reassurance that all is well.

Acceptance testing

When a program is first specified, we decide what behavior is expected out of it. Tests that are written to confirm that the program actually does what was expected are called acceptance tests. Acceptance tests can be written at any of the previously discussed levels, but most often you will see them at the integration or system level.

Acceptance tests tend to be the exception to the rule about progressing from unit tests to integration tests and then to system tests. Many program specifications describe the program at a fairly high level, and acceptance tests need to operate at the same level as that of the specification. It's not uncommon for the majority of system tests to be acceptance tests.

Acceptance tests are nice to have because they provide you with ongoing assurance that the program you're creating is actually the program that was specified.

Regression testing

A regression is when a part of your code that once functioned correctly stops doing so. Most often, that is a result of changes made elsewhere in the code undermining the assumptions of the now-buggy section. When this happens, it's a good idea to add tests to your test suite that can recognize the bug. This ensures that, if you ever make a similar mistake again, the test suite will catch it immediately.

Tests that make sure that the working code doesn't become buggy are called regression tests. They can be written before or after a bug is found, and they provide you with the assurance that your program's complexity is not causing the bugs to multiply. Once your code passes a unit test, integration test, or a system test, you don't need to delete these tests from the test suite. You can leave them in place, and they will function as additional regression tests, letting you know if the test stops working.

Test-driven development

When you combine all of the elements we've introduced in this chapter, you will arrive at the discipline of test-driven development. In test-driven development, you always write the tests first. Once you have tests for the code you're about to write, and only then, you will write the code that makes the tests pass.

This means that the first thing you will do is write the acceptance tests. Then you figure out which units of the program you're going to start with, and write tests—nominally, these are the regression tests, even though the bug they're catching at first is "the code doesn't exist"; this confirms that these units are not yet functioning correctly. Then you can write some code that makes the unit-level regression tests pass.

The process continues until the whole program is complete: write tests, then write code that makes the tests pass. If you discover a bug that isn't caught by an existing test, add a test first, then add or modify the code to make the test pass. The end result is a very solid program, thanks to all the bugs that were caught early, easily, and in less time.

You'll need Python

This book assumes that you have a working knowledge of the Python programming language, specifically, Version 3.4 or higher of that language. If you don't have Python already, you can download the complete language toolkit and library from `http://www.python.org/`, as a single easily-installed package.

> Most versions of Linux and Mac OS X already include Python, but not necessarily a new version that will work with this book. Run Python from the command line to check.

You'll also require your favorite text editor, preferably one that has language support for Python. Popular choices for editors include emacs, Vim, Geany, gedit, and Notepad++. For those willing to pay, TextMate and Sublime are popular.

> Some of these popular editors are somewhat... exotic. They have their own operating idiom, and don't behave like any other program you might have used. They're popular because they are highly functional; they may be weird, though. If you find that one editor doesn't suit you, just pick a different one.

Summary

In this chapter, we learned about what you can expect to learn from this book as well as talking a little bit about the philosophy of automated testing and test-driven development.

We talked about the different levels and roles of tests that combine to form a complete suite of tests for a program: unit tests, integration tests, system tests, acceptance tests, and regression tests. We learned that unit tests are the tests of the fundamental components of a program (such as functions); integration tests are the tests that cover larger swathes of a program (such as modules); system tests are the tests that cover a program in its entirety; acceptance tests make sure that the program is what it's supposed to be; and regression tests ensure that it keeps working as we develop it.

We talked about how automated testing can help you by moving the burden of testing mostly onto the computer. You can tell the computer how to check your code, instead of having to do the checks yourself. This makes it convenient to check your code early and more often, saves you from overlooking things you would otherwise miss, and helps you to quickly locate and fix bugs.

We talked about test-driven development, the discipline of writing your tests first, and letting them tell you what needs to be done in order to write the code you need. We also briefly discussed the development environment you'll require in order to work through this book.

Now, we're ready to move on to working with the `doctest` testing tool, the subject of the next chapter.

2

Working with doctest

The first testing tool we're going to look at is called `doctest`. The name is short for "document testing" or perhaps a "testable document". Either way, it's a literate tool designed to make it easy to write tests in such a way that computers and humans both benefit from them. Ideally, `doctest` tests both, informs human readers, and tells the computer what to expect.

Mixing tests and documentation helps us:

- Keeps the documentation up-to-date with reality
- Make sure that the tests express the intended behavior
- Reuse some of the efforts involved in the documentation and test creation

Where doctest performs best

The design decisions that went into `doctest` make it particularly well suited to writing acceptance tests at the integration and system testing levels. This is because `doctest` mixes human-only text with examples that both humans and computers can read. This structure doesn't support or enforce any of the formalizations of testing, but it conveys information beautifully and it still provides the computer with the ability to say *that works* or *that doesn't work*. As an added bonus, it is about the easiest way to write tests you'll ever see.

In other words, a `doctest` file is a truly excellent program specification that you can have the computer check against your actual code any time you want. API documentation also benefits from being written as doctests and checked alongside your other tests. You can even include doctests in your docstrings.

The basic idea you should be getting from all this is that `doctest` is ideal for uses where humans and computers will both benefit from reading them.

The doctest language

Like program source code, `doctest` tests are written in plain text. The `doctest` module extracts the tests and ignores the rest of the text, which means that the tests can be embedded in human-readable explanations or discussions. This is the feature that makes `doctest` suitable for uses such as program specifications.

Example – creating and running a simple doctest

We are going to create a simple `doctest` file, to show the fundamentals of using the tool. Perform the following steps:

1. Open a new text file in your editor, and name it `test.txt`.
2. Insert the following text into the file:

   ```
   This is a simple doctest that checks some of Python's arithmetic
   operations.

   >>> 2 + 2
   4

   >>> 3 * 3
   10
   ```

3. We can now run the `doctest`. At the command prompt, change to the directory where you saved `test.txt`. Type the following command:

   ```
   $ python3 -m doctest test.txt
   ```

4. When the test is run, you should see output like this:

   ```
   $ python3 -m doctest test.txt
   **********************************************************************
   File "test.txt", line 7, in test.txt
   Failed example:
       3 * 3
   Expected:
       10
   Got:
       9
   **********************************************************************
   1 items had failures:
      1 of   2 in test.txt
   ***Test Failed*** 1 failures.
   $
   ```

Result – three times three does not equal ten

You just wrote a `doctest` file that describes a couple of arithmetic operations, and ran it to check whether Python behaved as the tests said it should. You ran the tests by telling Python to execute `doctest` on the file containing the tests.

In this case, Python's behavior differed from the tests because, according to the tests, three times three equals ten. However, Python disagrees on that. As `doctest` expected one thing and Python did something different, `doctest` presented you with a nice little error report showing where to find the failed test, and how the actual result differed from the expected result. At the bottom of the report is a summary showing how many tests failed in each file tested, which is helpful when you have more than one file containing tests.

The syntax of doctests

You might have already figured it out from looking at the previous example: `doctest` recognizes tests by looking for sections of text that look like they've been copied and pasted from a Python interactive session. Anything that can be expressed in Python is valid within a `doctest`.

Lines that start with a `>>>` prompt are sent to a Python interpreter. Lines that start with a `...` prompt are sent as continuations of the code from the previous line, allowing you to embed complex block statements into your doctests. Finally, any lines that don't start with `>>>` or `...`, up to the next blank line or `>>>` prompt, represent the output expected from the statement. The output appears as it would in an interactive Python session, including both the return value and anything printed to the console. If you don't have any output lines, `doctest` assumes it to mean that the statement is expected to have no visible result on the console, which usually means that it returns None.

The `doctest` module ignores anything in the file that isn't part of a test, which means that you can put explanatory text, HTML, line-art diagrams, or whatever else strikes your fancy in between your tests. We took advantage of this in the previous `doctest` to add an explanatory sentence before the test itself.

Example – a more complex test

Add the following code to your `test.txt` file, separated from the existing code by at least one blank line:

```
Now we're going to take some more of doctest's syntax for a spin.

>>> import sys
```

```
>>> def test_write():
...     sys.stdout.write("Hello\n")
...     return True
>>> test_write()
Hello
True
```

Now take a moment to consider before running the test. Will it pass or fail? Should it pass or fail?

Result – five tests run

Just as we discussed before, run the test using the following command:

```
python3 -m doctest test.txt
```

You should see a result like this:

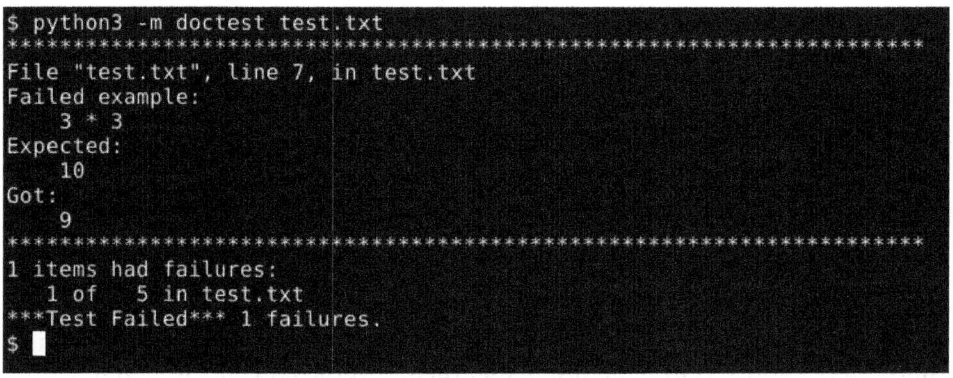

```
$ python3 -m doctest test.txt
**********************************************************************
File "test.txt", line 7, in test.txt
Failed example:
    3 * 3
Expected:
    10
Got:
    9
**********************************************************************
1 items had failures:
   1 of   5 in test.txt
***Test Failed*** 1 failures.
$
```

Because we added the new tests to the same file containing the tests from before, we still see the notification that three times three does not equal 10. Now, though, we also see that five tests were run, which means our new tests ran and were successful.

Why five tests? As far as `doctest` is concerned, we added the following three tests to the file:

- The first one says that, when we `import sys`, nothing visible should happen
- The second test says that, when we define the `test_write` function, nothing visible should happen
- The third test says that, when we call the `test_write` function, `Hello` and `True` should appear on the console, in that order, on separate lines

Since all three of these tests pass, `doctest` doesn't bother to say much about them. All it did was increase the number of tests reported at the bottom from two to five.

Expecting exceptions

That's all well and good for testing that things work as expected, but it is just as important to make sure that things fail when they're supposed to fail. Put another way: sometimes your code is supposed to raise an exception, and you need to be able to write tests that check that behavior as well.

Fortunately, `doctest` follows nearly the same principle in dealing with exceptions as it does with everything else; it looks for text that looks like a Python interactive session. This means it looks for text that looks like a Python exception report and traceback, and matches it against any exception that gets raised.

The `doctest` module does handle exceptions a little differently from the way it handles other things. It doesn't just match the text precisely and report a failure if it doesn't match. Exception tracebacks tend to contain many details that are not relevant to the test, but that can change unexpectedly. The `doctest` module deals with this by ignoring the traceback entirely: it's only concerned with the first line, `Traceback (most recent call last):`, which tells it that you expect an exception, and the part after the traceback, which tells it which exception you expect. The `doctest` module only reports a failure if one of these parts does not match.

This is helpful for a second reason as well: manually figuring out what the traceback will look like, when you're writing your tests, would require a significant amount of effort and would gain you nothing. It's better to simply omit them.

Example – checking for an exception

This is yet another test that you can add to `test.txt`, this time testing some code that ought to raise an exception.

Insert the following text into your `doctest` file, as always separated by at least one blank line:

```
Here we use doctest's exception syntax to check that Python is
correctly enforcing its grammar. The error is a missing ) on the def
line.

>>> def faulty(:
...     yield from [1, 2, 3, 4, 5]
Traceback (most recent call last):
SyntaxError: invalid syntax
```

The test is supposed to raise an exception, so it will fail if it doesn't raise the exception or if it raises the wrong exception. Make sure that you have your mind wrapped around this: if the test code executes successfully, the test fails, because it expected an exception.

Run the tests using the following doctest:

```
python3 -m doctest test.txt
```

Result – success at failing

The code contains a syntax error, which means this raises a `SyntaxError` exception, which in turn means that the example behaves as expected; this signifies that the test passes.

```
$ python3 -m doctest test.txt
**********************************************************************
File "test.txt", line 7, in test.txt
Failed example:
    3 * 3
Expected:
    10
Got:
    9
**********************************************************************
1 items had failures:
   1 of   6 in test.txt
***Test Failed*** 1 failures.
$ 
```

When dealing with exceptions, it is often desirable to be able to use a wildcard matching mechanism. The `doctest` provides this facility through its ellipsis directive that we'll discuss shortly.

Expecting blank lines

The `doctest` uses the first blank line after `>>>` to identify the end of the expected output, so what do you do when the expected output actually contains a blank line?

The `doctest` handles this situation by matching a line that contains only the text `<BLANKLINE>` in the expected output with a real blank line in the actual output.

Controlling doctest behavior with directives

Sometimes, the default behavior of `doctest` makes writing a particular test inconvenient. For example, `doctest` might look at a trivial difference between the expected and real outputs and wrongly conclude that the test has failed. This is where `doctest` directives come to the rescue. Directives are specially formatted comments that you can place after the source code of a test and that tell `doctest` to alter its default behavior in some way.

A directive comment begins with `# doctest:`, after which comes a comma-separated list of options that either enable or disable various behaviors. To enable a behavior, write a `+` (plus symbol) followed by the behavior name. To disable a behavior, white a `-` (minus symbol) followed by the behavior name. We'll take a look at the several directives in the following sections.

Ignoring part of the result

It's fairly common that only part of the output of a test is actually relevant to determining whether the test passes. By using the `+ELLIPSIS` directive, you can make `doctest` treat the text `...` (called an ellipsis) in the expected output as a wildcard that will match any text in the output.

When you use an ellipsis, `doctest` will scan until it finds text matching whatever comes after the ellipsis in the expected output, and continue matching from there. This can lead to surprising results such as an ellipsis matching against a 0-length section of the actual output, or against multiple lines. For this reason, it needs to be used thoughtfully.

Example – ellipsis test drive

We're going to use the ellipsis in a few different tests to better get a feel of how it works. As an added bonus, these tests also show the use of `doctest` directives.

Add the following code to your `test.txt` file:

```
Next up, we're exploring the ellipsis.

>>> sys.modules # doctest: +ELLIPSIS
{...'sys': <module 'sys' (built-in)>...}

>>> 'This is an expression that evaluates to a string'
... # doctest: +ELLIPSIS
```

```
'This is ... a string'

>>> 'This is also a string' # doctest: +ELLIPSIS
'This is ... a string'

>>> import datetime
>>> datetime.datetime.now().isoformat() # doctest: +ELLIPSIS
'...-...-...T...:...:...'
```

Result – ellipsis elides

The tests all pass, where they would all fail without the ellipsis. The first and last tests, in which we checked for the presence of a specific module in `sys.modules` and confirmed a specific formatting while ignoring the contents of a string, demonstrate the kind of situation where ellipsis is really useful, because it lets you focus on the part of the output that is meaningful and ignore the rest of the test. The middle tests demonstrate how different outputs can match the same expected result when ellipsis is in play.

Look at the last test. Can you imagine any output that wasn't an ISO-formatted time stamp, but that would match the example anyway? Remember that the ellipsis can match any amount of text.

Ignoring white space

Sometimes, white space (spaces, tabs, newlines, and their ilk) is more trouble than it's worth. Maybe you want to be able to break a single line of expected output across several lines in your test file, or maybe you're testing a system that uses lots of white space but doesn't convey any useful information with it.

The `doctest` gives you a way to "normalize" white space, turning any sequence of white space characters, in both the expected output and in the actual output, into a single space. It then checks whether these normalized versions match.

Example – invoking normality

We're going to write a couple of tests that demonstrate how whitespace normalization works.

Insert the following code into your `doctest` file:

```
Next, a demonstration of whitespace normalization.

>>> [1, 2, 3, 4, 5, 6, 7, 8, 9]
```

```
... # doctest: +NORMALIZE_WHITESPACE
[1, 2, 3,
 4, 5, 6,
 7, 8, 9]

>>> sys.stdout.write("This text\n contains weird     spacing.\n")
... # doctest: +NORMALIZE_WHITESPACE
This text contains weird spacing.
39
```

Result – white space matches any other white space

Both of these tests pass, in spite of the fact that the result of the first one has been wrapped across multiple lines to make it easy for humans to read, and the result of the second one has had its strange newlines and indentations left out, also for human convenience.

Notice how one of the tests inserts extra whitespace in the expected output, while the other one ignores extra whitespace in the actual output? When you use `+NORMALIZE_WHITESPACE`, you gain a lot of flexibility with regard to how things are formatted in the text file.

> You may have noted the value `39` on the last line of the last example. Why is that there? It's because the `write()` method returns the number of bytes that were written, which in this case happens to be `39`. If you're trying this example in an environment that maps ASCII characters to more than one byte, you will see a different number here; this will cause the test to fail until you change the expected number of bytes.

Skipping an example

On some occasions, `doctest` will recognize some text as an example to be checked, when in truth you want it to be simply text. This situation is rarer than it might at first seem, because usually there's no harm in letting `doctest` check everything it can. In fact, usually it's very helpful to have `doctest` check everything it can. For those times when you want to limit what `doctest` checks, though, there's the `+SKIP` directive.

Example – humans only

Append the following code to your doctest file:

```
Now we're telling doctest to skip a test

>>> 'This test would fail.' # doctest: +SKIP
If it were allowed to run.
```

Result – it looks like a test, but it's not

Before we added this last example to the file, `doctest` reported thirteen tests when we ran the file through it. After adding this code, `doctest` still reports thirteen tests. Adding the skip directive to the code completely removed it from consideration by doctest. It's not a test that passes, nor a test that fails. It's not a test at all.

The other directives

There are a number of other directives that can be issued to doctest, should you find the need. They're not as broadly useful as the ones already mentioned, but the time might come when you require one or more of them.

> The full documentation for all of the doctest directives can be found at `http://docs.python.org/3/library/doctest.html#doctest-options`.

The remaining directives of `doctest` in the Python 3.4 version are as follows:

- `DONT_ACCEPT_TRUE_FOR_1`: This makes `doctest` differentiate between boolean values and numbers
- `DONT_ACCEPT_BLANKLINE`: This removes support for the <BLANKLINE> feature
- `IGNORE_EXCEPTION_DETAIL`: This makes `doctest` only care that an exception is of the expected type

Strictly speaking, `doctest` supports several other options that can be set using the directive syntax, but they don't make any sense as directives, so we'll ignore them here.

The execution scope of doctest tests

When `doctest` is running the tests from text files, all the tests from the same file are run in the same execution scope. This means that, if you import a module or bind a variable in one test, that module or variable is still available in later tests. We took advantage of this fact several times in the tests written so far in this chapter: the `sys` module was only imported once, for example, although it was used in several tests.

This behavior is not necessarily beneficial, because tests need to be isolated from each other. We don't want them to contaminate each other because, if a test depends on something that another test does, or if it fails because of something that another test does, these two tests are in some sense combined into one test that covers a larger section of your code. You don't want that to happen, because then knowing which test has failed doesn't give you as much information about what went wrong and where it happened.

So, how can we give each test its own execution scope? There are a few ways to do it. One would be to simply place each test in its own file, along with whatever explanatory text that is needed. This works well in terms of functionality, but running the tests can be a pain unless you have a tool to find and run all of them for you. We'll talk about one such tool (called Nose) in a later chapter. Another problem with this approach is that this breaks the idea that the tests contribute to a human-readable document.

Another way to give each test its own execution scope is to define each test within a function, as follows:

```
>>> def test1():
...     import frob
...     return frob.hash('qux')
>>> test1()
77
```

By doing this, the only thing that ends up in the shared scope is the test function (named `test1` here). The `frob` module and any other names bound inside the function are isolated with the caveat that things that happen inside imported modules are not isolated. If the `frob.hash()` method changes a state inside the `frob` module, that state will still be changed if a different test imports the `frob` module again.

The third way is to exercise caution with the names you create, and be sure to set them to known values at the beginning of each test section. In many ways this is the easiest approach, but this is also the one that places the most burden on you, because you have to keep track of what's in the scope.

Why does `doctest` behave in this way, instead of isolating tests from each other? The `doctest` files are intended not just for computers to read, but also for humans. They often form a sort of narrative, flowing from one thing to the next. It would break the narrative to be constantly repeating what came before. In other words, this approach is a compromise between being a document and being a test framework, a middle ground that works for both humans and computers.

The other framework that we will study in depth in this book (called simply `unittest`) works at a more formal level, and enforces the separation between tests.

Check your understanding

Once you've decided on your answers to these questions, check them by writing a test document and running it through `doctest`:

- How does `doctest` recognize the beginning of a test in a document?
- How does `doctest` know when a test continues to further lines?
- How does `doctest` recognize the beginning and end of the expected output of a test?
- How would you tell `doctest` that you want to break the expected output across several lines, even though that's not how the test actually outputs it?
- Which parts of an exception report are ignored by `doctest`?
- When you assign a variable in a test file, which parts of the file can actually *see* that variable?
- Why do we care what code can *see* the variables created by a test?
- How can we make `doctest` not care what a section of output contains?

Exercise – English to doctest

Time to stretch your wings a bit. I'm going to give you a description of a single function in English. Your job is to copy the description into a new text file, and then add tests that describe all the requirements in a way that the computer can understand and check.

Try to make the doctests so that they're not just for the computer. Good doctests tend to clarify things for human readers as well. By and large, this means that you present them to human readers as examples interspersed with the text.

Without further ado, here is the English description:

```
The fib(N) function takes a single integer as its only parameter N.
If N is 0 or 1, the function returns 1. If N is less than 0, the
function raises a ValueError. Otherwise, the function returns the sum
of fib(N - 1) and fib(N - 2). The returned value will never be less
than 1. A naïve implementation of this function would get very slow as
N increased.
```

I'll give you a hint and point out that the last sentence about the function being slow, isn't really testable. As computers get faster, any test you write that depends on an arbitrary definition of "slow" will eventually fail. Also, there's no good way to test the difference between a slow function and a function stuck in an infinite loop, so there's not much point in trying. If you find yourself needing to do that, it's best to back off and try a different solution.

> Not being able to tell whether a function is stuck or just slow is called the halting problem by computer scientists. We know that it can't be solved unless we someday discover a fundamentally better kind of computer. Faster computers won't do the trick, and neither will quantum computers, so don't hold your breath.

The next-to-last sentence also provides some difficulty, since to test it completely would require running every positive integer through the `fib()` function, which would take forever (except that the computer will eventually run out of memory and force Python to raise an exception). How do we deal with this sort of thing, then?

The best solution is to check whether the condition holds true for a random sample of viable inputs. The `random.randrange()` and `random.choice()` functions in the Python standard library make that fairly easy to do.

Embedding doctests into docstrings

It's just as easy to write doctests into docstrings as it is to write them into documentation files.

> For those who don't know, docstrings are a Python feature that allows programmers to embed documentation directly into their source code. The Python `help()` function is powered by docstrings. To learn more about docstrings, you can start with the Python tutorial section at `https://docs.python.org/3/tutorial/controlflow.html#documentation-strings`.

When written in docstrings, doctests serve a slightly different purpose. They still let the computer check that things work as expected, but the humans who see them will most often be coders who use the Python interactive shell to work on an idea before committing it to code, or whose text editor pops up docstrings as they work. In that context, the most important thing a `doctest` can do is be informative, so docstrings aren't usually a good place for checking picky details. They're a great place for a `doctest` to demonstrate the proper behavior of a common case, though.

The doctests embedded in docstrings have a somewhat different execution scope than doctests in text files do. Instead of having a single scope for all of the tests in the file, `doctest` creates a single scope for each docstring. All of the tests that share a docstring also share an execution scope, but they're isolated from tests in the other docstrings.

The separation of each docstring into its own execution scope often means that we don't need to put much thought into isolating doctests when they're embedded in docstrings. This is fortunate, since docstrings are primarily intended for documentation, and the tricks required to isolate the tests might obscure the meaning.

Example – a doctest in a docstring

We're going to embed a test right inside the Python source file that it tests, by placing it inside a docstring.

Create a file called `test.py` containing the following code:

```
def testable(x):
    r"""
    The `testable` function returns the square root of its
    parameter, or 3, whichever is larger.

    >>> testable(7)
    3.0

    >>> testable(16)
    4.0

    >>> testable(9)
    3.0

    >>> testable(10) == 10 ** 0.5
    True
    """
    if x < 9:
        return 3.0
    return x ** 0.5
```

> Notice the use of a raw string for the docstring (denoted by the `r` character before the first triple quote). Using raw strings for your docstrings is a good habit to get into, because you usually don't want escape sequences—for example, `\n` for newline— to be interpreted by the Python interpreter. You want them to be treated as text, so that they are correctly passed on to doctest.

Running these tests is just as easy as running the tests in a doctest document:

```
python3 -m doctest test.py
```

Since all the tests pass, the output of this command is nothing at all. We can make it more interesting by adding the verbose flag to the command line:

```
python3 -m doctest -v test.py
```

Result – the code is now self-documenting and self-testable

When we run the Python file through `doctest` with the verbose flag, we see the output, as shown in the the following screenshot:

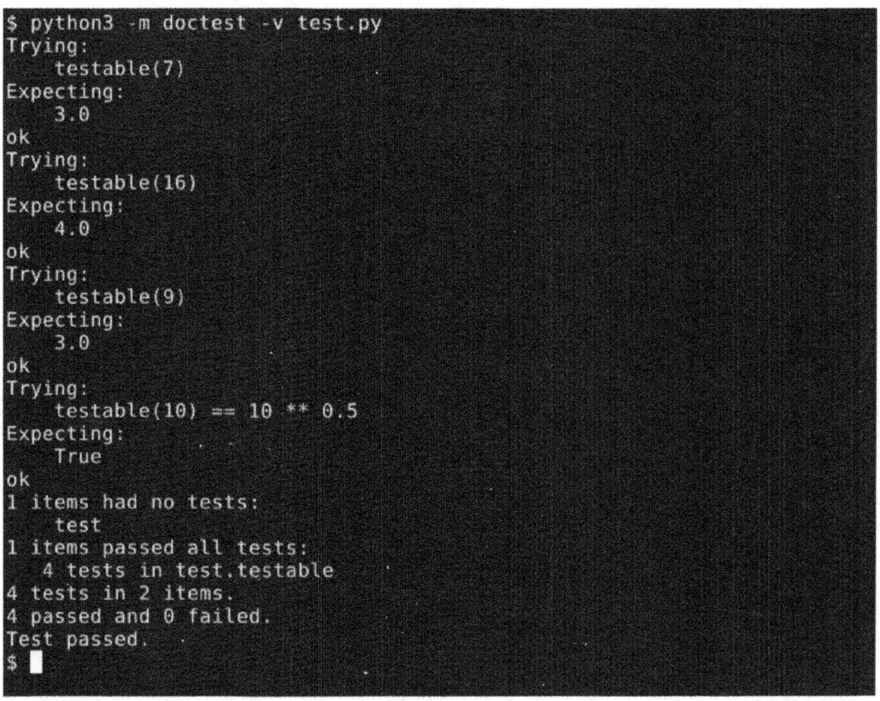

We put the `doctest` code right inside the docstring of the function it was testing. This is a good place for tests that also show a programmer how to do something. It's not a good place for detailed, low-level tests (the `doctest` in the docstring example code, which was quite detailed for illustrative purposes, is perhaps too detailed), because docstrings need to serve as API documentation—you can see the reason for this just by looking at the example, where the doctests take up most of the room in the docstring without telling the readers any more than they would have learned from a single test.

Any test that will serve as good API documentation is a good candidate for including in the docstrings of a Python file.

You might be wondering about the line that reads `1 items had no tests`, and the following line that just reads `test`. These lines are referring to the fact that there are no tests written in the module-level docstring. That's a little surprising, since we didn't include such a docstring in our source code at all, until you realize that, as far as Python (and thus `doctest`) is concerned, no docstring is the same as an empty docstring.

Putting it into practice – an AVL tree

We're going to walk step-by-step through the process of using `doctest` to create a testable specification for a data structure called an AVL tree. An AVL tree is a way to organize key-value pairs so that they can be quickly located by key. In other words, it's a lot like Python's built-in dictionary type. The name AVL references the initials of the people who invented this data structure.

> While AVL trees are similar to Python dictionaries, they have some significantly different properties. For one thing, the keys stored in an AVL tree can be iterated over in a sorted order with no overhead. Another difference is that, while inserting and removing objects in an AVL tree is slower than a Python `dict` in many cases, it's faster in the worst case.

As its name suggests, an AVL tree organizes the keys that are stored in it into a tree structure, with each key having up to two child keys —one child key that is less than the parent key by comparison, and one that is more. In the following figure, the `Elephant` key has two child keys, `Goose` has one, and `Aardvark` and `Frog` both have none.

The AVL tree is special because it keeps one side of the tree from getting much taller than the other, which means that users can expect it to perform reliably and efficiently no matter what. In the following figure, the AVL tree will reorganize to stay balanced if `Frog` gains a child:

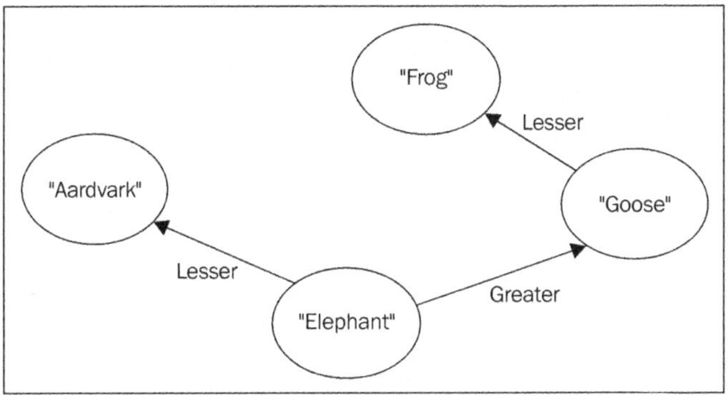

We're going to write tests for an AVL tree implementation here, rather than writing the implementation itself, so we're going to gloss over the details of *how* an AVL tree works, in favor of looking at what it should do when it works right.

> If you want to know more about AVL trees, you will find many good references on the Internet. Wikipedia's entry on this subject is a good place to start with: `http://en.wikipedia.org/wiki/AVL_tree`.

We're going to start with a plain-language specification, and then interject tests between the paragraphs. You don't have to actually type all of this into a text file; it is here for you to read and to think about.

English specification

The first step is to describe what the desired result should be, in normal language. This might be something that you do for yourself, or it might be something that somebody else does for you. If you're working for somebody, hopefully you and your employer can sit down together and work this part out.

In this case, there's not much to work out, because AVL trees have been fully described for decades. Even so, the description here isn't quite like the one you'd find elsewhere. This capacity for ambiguity is exactly the reason why a plain-language specification isn't good enough. We need an unambiguous specification, and that's exactly what the tests in a doctest file can give us.

The following text goes in a file called `AVL.txt`, (that you can find in its final form in the accompanying code archive; at this stage of the process, the file contains only the normal language specification):

```
An AVL Tree consists of a collection of nodes organized in a binary
tree structure. Each node has left and right children, each of which
may be either None or another tree node. Each node has a key, which
must be comparable via the less-than operator. Each node has a value.
Each node also has a height number, measuring how far the node is from
being a leaf of the tree -- a node with height 0 is a leaf.

The binary tree structure is maintained in ordered form, meaning that
of a node's two children, the left child has a key that compares
less than the node's key and the right child has a key that compares
greater than the node's key.

The binary tree structure is maintained in a balanced form, meaning
that for any given node, the heights of its children are either the
same or only differ by 1.

The node constructor takes either a pair of parameters representing
a key and a value, or a dict object representing the key-value pairs
with which to initialize a new tree.

The following methods target the node on which they are called, and
can be considered part of the internal mechanism of the tree:

Each node has a recalculate_height method, which correctly sets the
height number.

Each node has a make_deletable method, which exchanges the positions
of the node and one of its leaf descendants, such that the tree
ordering of the nodes remains correct.

Each node has rotate_clockwise and rotate_counterclockwise methods.
Rotate_clockwise takes the node's right child and places it where
the node was, making the node into the left child of its own former
child. Other nodes in the vicinity are moved so as to maintain
the tree ordering. The opposite operation is performed by rotate_
counterclockwise.

Each node has a locate method, taking a key as a parameter, which
searches the node and its descendants for a node with the specified
key, and either returns that node or raises a KeyError.

The following methods target the whole tree rooted at the current
node. The intent is that they will be called on the root node:
```

```
Each node has a get method taking a key as a parameter, which locates
the value associated with the specified key and returns it, or raises
KeyError if the key is not associated with any value in the tree.

Each node has a set method taking a key and a value as parameters, and
associating the key and value within the tree.

Each node has a remove method taking a key as a parameter, and
removing the key and its associated value from the tree. It raises
KeyError if no value was associated with that key.
```

Node data

The first three paragraphs of the specification describe the member variables of an AVL tree node, and tell us what the valid values for the variables are. They also tell us how the tree height should be measured and define what a balanced tree means. It's our job now to take these ideas, and encode them into tests that the computer can eventually use to check our code.

We can check these specifications by creating a node and then testing the values, but that would really just be a test of the constructor. It's important to test the constructor, but what we really want to do is to incorporate checks that the node variables are left in a valid state into our tests of each member function.

To that end, we'll define functions that our tests can call to check that the state of a node is valid. We'll define these functions just after the third paragraph, because they provide extra details related to the content of the first three paragraphs:

> Notice that the node data test is written as if the AVL tree implementation already existed. It tries to import an `avl_tree` module containing an AVL class, and it tries to use the AVL class in specific ways. Of course, at the moment there is no `avl_tree` module, so the tests will fail. This is as it should be. All that the failure means is that, when the time comes to implement the tree, we should do so in a module called `avl_tree`, with contents that function as our tests assume. Part of the benefit of testing like this is being able to test-drive your code before you even write it.

```
>>> from avl_tree import AVL

>>> def valid_state(node):
...     if node is None:
...         return
...     if node.left is not None:
```

```
...             assert isinstance(node.left, AVL)
...             assert node.left.key < node.key
...             left_height = node.left.height + 1
...         else:
...             left_height = 0
...
...         if node.right is not None:
...             assert isinstance(node.right, AVL)
...             assert node.right.key > node.key
...             right_height = node.right.height + 1
...         else:
...             right_height = 0
...
...         assert abs(left_height - right_height) < 2
...         node.key < node.key
...         node.value

>>> def valid_tree(node):
...     if node is None:
...         return
...     valid_state(node)
...     valid_tree(node.left)
...     valid_tree(node.right)
```

Notice that we didn't actually call these functions yet. They aren't tests, as such, but tools that we'll use to simplify writing tests. We define them here, rather than in the Python module that we're going to test, because they aren't conceptually part of the tested code, and because anyone who reads the tests will need to be able to see what the helper functions do.

Testing the constructor

The fourth paragraph describes the constructor of the AVL class. According to this paragraph, the constructor has two modes of operation: it can create a single initialized node, or it can create and initialize a whole tree of nodes based on the contents of a dictionary.

The test for the single node mode is easy. We'll add it after the fourth paragraph:

```
>>> valid_state(AVL(2, 'Testing is fun'))
```

We don't even have to write an expected result, since we wrote the function to raise an `AssertionError` if there's a problem and to return None if everything is fine. `AssertionError` is triggered by the `assert` statement in our test code, if the expression in the `assert` statement produces a false value.

The test for the second mode looks just as easy, and we'll add it right after the other:

```
>>> valid_tree(AVL({1: 'Hello', 2: 'World', -3: '!'}))
```

There's a bit of buried complexity here, though. In all probability, this constructor will function by initializing a single node and then using that node's `set` method to add the rest of the keys and values to the tree. This means that our second constructor test isn't a unit test, it's an integration test that checks the interaction of multiple units.

Specification documents often contains integration-level and system-level tests, so this isn't really a problem. It's something to be aware of, though, because if this test fails it won't necessarily show you where the problem really lies. Your unit tests will do that.

Something else to notice is that we didn't check whether the constructor fails appropriately when given bad inputs. These tests are very important, but the English specification didn't mention these points at all, which means that they're not really among the acceptance criteria. We'll add these tests to the unit test suite instead.

Recalculating height

The `recalculate_height()` method is described in the fifth paragraph of the specification. To test it, we're going to need a tree for it to operate on, and we don't want to use the second mode of the constructor to create it —after all, we want this test to be independent of any errors that might exist there. We'd really prefer to make the test entirely independent of the constructor but, in this case, we need to make a small exception to the rule, since it's mighty difficult to create an object without calling its constructor in some way.

What we're going to do is define a function that builds a specific tree and returns it. This function will be useful in several of our later tests as well:

```
>>> def make_test_tree():
...     root = AVL(7, 'seven')
...     root.height = 2
...     root.left = AVL(3, 'three')
...     root.left.height = 1
...     root.left.right = AVL(4, 'four')
...     root.right = AVL(10, 'ten')
...     return root
```

Now that we have the make_test_tree() function, testing recalculate_height() is easy:

```
>>> tree = make_test_tree()
>>> tree.height = 0
>>> tree.recalculate_height()
>>> tree.height
2
```

Making a node deletable

The sixth paragraph of the specification described the make_deletable() method. You can't delete a node that has children, because that would leave the node's children disconnected from the rest of the tree. Consider the tree with animal names in it that we looked at earlier. If we delete the Elephant node from the bottom of the tree, what do we do about Aardvark, Goose, and Frog? If we delete Goose, how do we find Frog afterwards?

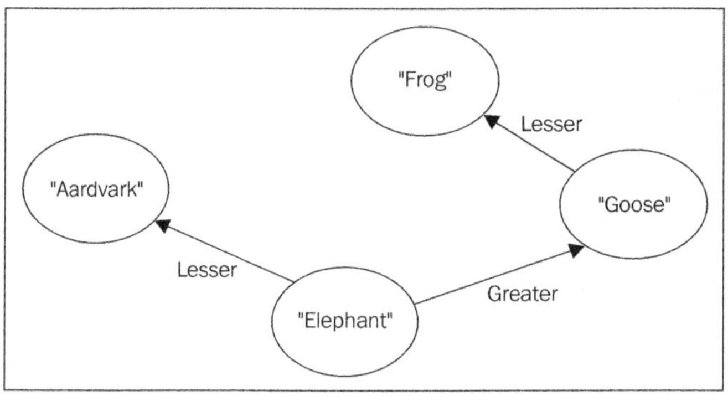

The way around that is to have the node swap places with its largest leaf descendant on the left side (or its smallest leaf descendant on the right side, but we're not doing it that way).

We'll test this by using the same make_test_tree() function that we defined earlier to create a new tree to work on, and then check whether make_deletable() swaps correctly:

```
>>> tree = make_test_tree()
>>> target = tree.make_deletable()
>>> (tree.value, tree.height)
('four', 2)
>>> (target.value, target.height)
('seven', 0)
```

Rotation

The two rotate functions, described in paragraph seven of the specification, perform a somewhat tricky manipulation of the links in a tree. You probably found the plain language description of what they do a bit confusing. This is one of those times when a little bit of code makes a whole lot more sense than any number of sentences.

While tree rotation is usually defined in terms of rearranging the links between nodes in the tree, we'll check whether it worked by looking at the values rather than by looking directly at the left and right links. This allows the implementation to swap the contents of nodes, rather than the nodes themselves, when it wishes. After all, it's not important to the specification which operation happens, so we shouldn't rule out a perfectly reasonable implementation choice:

```
>>> tree = make_test_tree()
>>> tree.value
'seven'
>>> tree.left.value
'three'
>>> tree.rotate_counterclockwise()
>>> tree.value
'three'
>>> tree.left is None
True
>>> tree.right.value
'seven'
>>> tree.right.left.value
'four'
>>> tree.right.right.value
'ten'
>>> tree.right.left.value
'four'
>>> tree.left is None
True

>>> tree.rotate_clockwise()
>>> tree.value
'seven'
>>> tree.left.value
'three'
>>> tree.left.right.value
'four'
>>> tree.right.value
'ten'
>>> tree.right.left is None
True
>>> tree.left.left is None
True
```

Locating a node

According to the eighth paragraph of the specification, the `locate()` method is expected to return a node, or raise a `KeyError` exception, depending on whether the key exists in the tree or not. We'll use our specially built testing tree again, so that we know exactly what the tree's structure looks like:

```
>>> tree = make_test_tree()
>>> tree.locate(4).value
'four'
>>> tree.locate(17) # doctest: +ELLIPSIS
Traceback (most recent call last):
KeyError: ...
```

> **Downloading the example code**
>
> You can download the example code files for all Packt books you have purchased from your account at `http://www.packtpub.com`. If you purchased this book elsewhere, you can visit `http://www.packtpub.com/support` and register to have the files e-mailed directly to you.

The rest of the specification

The remaining paragraphs of the specification describe higher-level functions that operate by calling the already described functions. This means that, until we learn the tricks of mock objects in *Chapter 4, Decoupling Units with unittest.mock*, we're stuck with writing integration-level tests here. As I mentioned earlier, this is not a terrible thing to do in a specification document, so we'll go ahead and do it:

```
Each node has a get method taking a key as a parameter, which locates
the value associated with the specified key and returns it, or raises
KeyError if the key is not associated with any value in the tree.

>>> tree = make_test_tree()
>>> tree.get(10)
'ten'
>>> tree.get(97) # doctest: +ELLIPSIS
Traceback (most recent call last):
KeyError: ...

Each node has a set method taking a key and a value as parameters, and
associating the key and value within the tree.
```

```
>>> tree = make_test_tree()
>>> tree.set(10, 'foo')
>>> tree.locate(10).value
'foo'

Each node has a remove method taking a key as a parameter, and
removing the key and its associated value from the tree. It raises
KeyError if no values was associated with that key.

>>> tree = make_test_tree()
>>> tree.remove(3)
>>> tree.remove(3) # doctest: +ELLIPSIS
Traceback (most recent call last):
KeyError: ...
```

Summary

We learned the syntax of `doctest`, and went through several examples describing how to use it. After that, we took a real-world specification for the AVL tree, and examined how to formalize it as a set of doctests, so that we could use it to automatically check the correctness of an implementation.

Specifically, we covered doctest's default syntax and the directives that alter it, how to write doctests in text files, how to write doctests in Python docstrings, and what it feels like to use `doctest` to turn a specification into tests.

Now that we've learned about `doctest`, we're ready to talk about how to use `doctest` to do unit testing—the topic of the next chapter.

3
Unit Testing with doctest

In the last chapter, we talked about what `doctest` does, how it works, and what you can expect out of it. Why are we devoting another chapter to it?

We're not. This chapter isn't really about `doctest`. It's about the testing discipline called **unit testing**. Since unit testing is an idea, not a piece of software, we'll be using `doctest` to practice with it.

In this chapter, we're going to see:

- What unit testing actually is
- How unit testing helps
- How `doctest` relates to unit testing

What is unit testing?

First of all, why do we care what unit testing is? One answer is that unit testing is a best practice that has been evolving toward its current form over most of the time that programming has existed. Another answer is that the core principles of unit testing are just good sense. It might actually be a little embarrassing to our community as a whole that it took us so long to recognize this.

So what is it? Unit testing means testing the smallest meaningful pieces of code (such pieces are called units), in such a way that guarantees that the success or failure of each test depends only on the unit and nothing else.

There's a reason for each part of this definition:

- We test the smallest meaningful pieces of code so that failed tests tell us where the problem is. The larger the tested chunk of code, the larger the area where a problem might originate.
- We make sure that each test depends only on the tested unit for success or failure because, if it invokes any code outside the unit, we can't guarantee that the test's success or failure is actually due to that unit. When tests aren't independent, you can't trust them to tell you what the problem is and where to find it.

We made some efforts to write our tests in *Chapter 2, Working with doctest*, according to this discipline, although we allowed ourselves some wiggle room because we were focusing on writing a testable specification. In this chapter, we're going to be more rigorous.

Automated testing is often associated with unit testing. Automated testing makes it fast and easy to run unit tests, and unit tests tend to be amenable to automation. We're certainly going to make heavy use of automated testing, both with `doctest` now, and later with tools such as unittest and Nose as well. However, strictly speaking, unit testing is not tied to automated testing. You can do unit testing with nothing but your own code and some discipline.

The limitations of unit testing

Any test that involves more than one unit is automatically not a unit test. That matters because the results of unit tests tend to be particularly clear about what a problem is and where to find it.

When you test multiple units at once, the results of the various units get mixed together. In the end, you have to wonder about both what the problem is (is the mistake in this piece of code, or is it correctly handling bad input from some other piece of code?), and where the problem is (this output is wrong, but how do the involved units work together to create the error?).

Empirical scientists must perform experiments that check only one hypothesis at a time, whether the subject at hand is Chemistry, Physics, or the behavior of a body of program code.

Example – identifying units

Imagine for a moment that one of your coworkers has written the following code, and it's your responsibility to test it:

```
class Testable:
    def method1(self, number):
        number += 4
        number **= 0.5
        number *= 7
        return number

    def method2(self, number):
        return ((number * 2) ** 1.27) * 0.3

    def method3(self, number):
        return self.method1(number) + self.method2(number)

    def method4(self):
        return 1.713 * self.method3(id(self))
```

Here are some things to think about: Which sections of this code are the units? Is there only one unit consisting of the entire class? Is each method a separate unit? What about each statement, or maybe each expression?

In some sense, the answer is subjective because part of the definition of a unit is that it is meaningful. You can say that the whole class is a single unit, and in some circumstances that might be the best answer. However, it is easy to subdivide most classes into methods, and normally methods make better units because they have well-defined interfaces and partially isolated behaviors, and because their intent and meaning should be well understood.

Statements and expressions don't make good units because they are almost never particularly meaningful in isolation. Furthermore, statements and expressions are difficult to target: unlike classes and methods, they don't have names or easy ways to focus a test on them.

Here are some things to think about: What will be the consequences of choosing a different definition of unit for this code? If you have decided that methods are the best units, what would be different if you had picked classes? Likewise, if you picked classes, what would be different if you'd picked methods?

Here are some things to think about: Take a look at `method4`. The result of this method depends on all of the other methods working correctly; worse, it depends on the unique ID of the self object. Can `method4` be treated as a unit? If we could change anything except `method4`, what is that we have to change to allow it to be tested as a unit and produce a predictable result?

Choosing units

You can't organize a suite of unit tests until you decide what constitutes a unit. The capabilities of your chosen programming language affect this choice. For example, C++ and Java make it difficult or impossible to treat methods as units (because you can't access a method without first instantiating the class it's part of); thus, in these languages each class is usually treated as a single unit, or metaprogramming tricks are used to force the methods into isolation so that they can be tested as units. C, on the other hand, doesn't support classes as language features at all, so the obvious choice of unit is the function. Python is flexible enough that either classes or methods can be considered as units and, of course, it has standalone functions as well; it is also natural to think of them as units.

The smaller the units are, the more useful the tests tend to be because they narrow down the location and nature of bugs more quickly. For example, if you choose to treat the `Testable` class as a unit, tests of the class will fail if there is a mistake in any of the methods. This tells you that there's a mistake in `Testable`, but not that it's in `method2`, or wherever it actually is. On the other hand, there is a certain amount of rigamarole involved in treating `method4` and its like as units, to such an extent that the next chapter of the book is dedicated to dealing with such situations. Even so, I recommend using methods and functions as units most of the time because it pays off in the long run.

When you were thinking about `method4`, you probably realized that the function calls to `id` and `self.method3` were the problem, and that the method can be tested as a unit if they didn't invoke other units. In Python, replacing the functions with stand-ins at runtime is fairly easy to do, and we'll be discussing a structured approach to this in the next chapter.

Check your understanding

Take a look at the code for this simple class, and use it to figure out the answers to the questions. It's okay to check back through the book. This is just a way for you to make sure you're ready to move on:

```
class ClassOne:
    def __init__(self, arg1, arg2):
        self.arg1 = int(arg1)
        self.arg2 = arg2

    def method1(self, x):
        return x * self.arg1

    def method2(self, x):
        return self.method1(self.arg2) * x
```

Here are the questions:

1. Assuming that we're using methods as units, how many units exist in the preceding code?

   Answer: There are three units that exist in the preceding code and that are as follows: `__init__`, `method1`, and `method2`. `__init__` is a method, just as `method1` and `method2`. The fact that it's a constructor means that it's all tangled up with the other units, but it's still a method containing code and a possible location for bugs, and so we cannot afford to treat this as anything other than a unit.

2. Which units make assumptions about the correct operation of other units? In other words, which units are not independent?

   Answer: Both `method1` and `method2` assume that `__init__` works right, and `method2` makes the same assumption as that of `method1`.

3. How can you write a test for `method2` that does not assume that other units work correctly?

   Answer: The tests for `method2` will need to use a fake `method1` that is a part of the test code, and not a part of the code being tested.

Unit testing during the development process

We're going to walk through the development of one class, treating it as a complete programming project and integrating unit testing at each step of the process. For something as small as a single standalone class, this may seem silly, but it illustrates the practices that keep larger projects from getting bogged down in a tangle of bugs.

We're going to create a PID controller class. A PID controller is a tool from control theory, a way of controlling machines so that they move smoothly and efficiently. The robot arms that assemble cars in factories are controlled by PID controllers. We'll be using a PID controller for this demonstration because it's a very useful, and a very real-world idea. Many programmers have been asked to implement PID controllers at some point in their careers. This example is meant to be read as if we are contractors and are being paid to produce results.

> If you find that the PID controllers are more interesting than simply an example in a programming book, wikipedia's article is a good place to begin learning about this: `http://en.wikipedia.org/wiki/PID_controller`.

Design

Our imaginary client gives us the following specification:

> *We want a class that implements a PID controller for a single variable. The measurement, setpoint and output should all be real numbers.*
>
> *We need to be able to adjust the setpoint at runtime, but we want it to have a memory, so we can easily return to the previous setpoint.*

We'll take this and make it more formal, not to mention complete, by writing a set of acceptance tests as unit tests that describe the behavior. This way we'll at least have it set down precisely as what we believe the client intended.

We need to write a set of tests that describe the constructor. After looking up what a PID controller actually is, we have learned that they are defined by three gains and a setpoint. The controller has three components: proportional, integral, and derivative (this is where the name PID comes from). Each gain is a number that determines how much effect one of the three parts of the controller has on the final result. The setpoint determines what the goal of the controller is; in other words, to where it's trying to move the controlled variable. Looking at all this, we decide that the constructor should just store the gains and the setpoint along with initializing some internal state that we know we'll need because we read about PID controllers. With this, we know enough to write some constructor tests:

```
>>> import pid

>>> controller = pid.PID(P=0.5, I=0.5, D=0.5, setpoint=0)

>>> controller.gains
(0.5, 0.5, 0.5)
>>> controller.setpoint
[0.0]
>>> controller.previous_time is None
True
>>> controller.previous_error
0.0
>>> controller.integrated_error
0.0
```

We also need tests that describe measurement processing. This means testing the actual use of the controller, taking a measured value as its input, and producing a control signal that should smoothly move the measured variable toward the setpoint.

The behavior of a PID controller is based on time; we know that, so we're going to need to be able to feed the controller time values that we choose if we expect the tests to produce predictable results. We do this by replacing `time.time` with a different function of the same signature, which produces predictable results.

Once we have that taken care of, we plug our test input values into the math that defines a PID controller along with the gains to figure out what the correct outputs will be, and use these numbers to write the tests:

```
Replace time.time with a predictable fake
>>> import time
>>> real_time = time.time
>>> time.time = (float(x) for x in range(1, 1000)).__next__

Make sure we're not inheriting old state from the constructor tests
>>> import imp
>>> pid = imp.reload(pid)

Actual tests. These test values are nearly arbitrary, having been
chosen for no reason other than that they should produce easily
recognized values.
>>> controller = pid.PID(P=0.5, I=0.5, D=0.5, setpoint=0)
>>> controller.calculate_response(12)
-6.0
>>> controller.calculate_response(6)
-3.0
>>> controller.calculate_response(3)
-4.5
>>> controller.calculate_response(-1.5)
-0.75
>>> controller.calculate_response(-2.25)
-1.125

Undo the fake
>>> time.time = real_time
```

We need to write tests that describe setpoint handling. Our client asked for a "memory" for setpoints, which we'll interpret as a stack, so we write tests that ensure that the setpoint stack works. Writing code that uses this stack behavior brings to our attention the fact that a PID controller with no setpoint is not a meaningful entity, so we add a test that checks that the PID class rejects this situation by raising an exception:

```
>>> pid = imp.reload(pid)
>>> controller = pid.PID(P = 0.5, I = 0.5, D = 0.5, setpoint = 0)
```

```
>>> controller.push_setpoint(7)
>>> controller.setpoint
[0.0, 7.0]

>>> controller.push_setpoint(8.5)
>>> controller.setpoint
[0.0, 7.0, 8.5]

>>> controller.pop_setpoint()
8.5
>>> controller.setpoint
[0.0, 7.0]

>>> controller.pop_setpoint()
7.0
>>> controller.setpoint
[0.0]

>>> controller.pop_setpoint()
Traceback (most recent call last):
ValueError: PID controller must have a setpoint
```

PID controllers are well-defined elsewhere, so the sparse specification that our client gave us works pretty well over all. Still, we had to codify several assumptions when we wrote our acceptance tests; it would probably be wise to check with the client and make sure that we didn't go astray, which means that, before we even ran the tests, they already helped us by pointing out questions we needed to ask them.

We took extra steps in the tests to help isolate them from each other, by forcing the `pid` module to reimport before each group of test statements. This has the effect of resetting anything that might have changed in the module, and causes it to reimport any modules that it depends on. This is particularly important, since we replaced `time.time` with a dummy function. We want to be sure that the `pid` module uses the dummy time function, so we reload the `pid` module. If the real-time function is used instead of the dummy, the test won't be useful because it will succeed only once. Tests need to be repeatable.

The stand-in time function was created by making an iterator that counts through the integers from 1 to 999 (as floating point values), and binding `time.time` to that iterator's `__next__` method. Once we were done with the time-dependent tests, we replaced the original `time.time`.

We did get a little bit lazy, though, because we didn't bother to isolate the assorted tests from the PID constructor. If there's a bug in the constructor, it might cause a false error report in any of the tests that are dependent on it. We could have been more rigorous by using a mock object instead of an actual PID object, and thus even skipped invoking the constructor during the tests of other units but, as we aren't talking about mock objects until the next chapter, we'll allow ourselves a bit of laziness here.

Right now, we have tests for a module that doesn't exist. That's good! Writing the tests was easier than writing the module, and this gives us a stepping stone towards getting the module right, quickly and easily. As a general rule, you always want to have tests ready before the code that the test is written for.

> Note that I said "you want to have tests ready," not "you want to have all of the tests ready." You don't want, or need, to have every test in place before you start writing code. What you want is to have the tests in place that define the things you already know at the start of the process.

Development

Now that we have some tests, we can begin writing code to satisfy the tests, and thus also the specification.

> What if the code is already written? We can still write tests for its units. This isn't as productive as writing the tests in parallel with the code, but this at least gives us a way to check our assumptions and make sure that we don't introduce regressions. A test suite written late is better than no test suite at all.

The first step is to run the tests because this is always the first thing you do when you need to decide what to do next. If all the tests pass, either you're done with the program or you need to write more tests. If one or more tests fail, you pick one and make it pass.

So, we run the tests as follows:

```
python3 -m doctest PID.txt
```

The first time they tell us that we don't have a `pid` module. Let's create one and fill it with a first attempt at a `PID` class:

```
from time import time

class PID:
    def __init__(self, P, I, D, setpoint):
        self.gains = (float(P), float(I), float(D))
        self.setpoint = [float(setpoint)]
        self.previous_time = None
        self.previous_error = 0.0
        self.integrated_error = 0.0

    def push_setpoint(self, target):
        self.setpoint.append(float(target))

    def pop_setpoint(self):
        if len(self.setpoint) > 1:
            return self.setpoint.pop()
        raise ValueError('PID controller must have a setpoint')

    def calculate_response(self, value):
        now = time()
        P, I, D = self.gains

        err = value - self.setpoint[-1]

        result = P * err
        if self.previous_time is not None:
            delta = now - self.previous_time
            self.integrated_error += err * delta
            result += I * self.integrated_error
            result += D * (err - self.previous_error) / delta

        self.previous_error = err
        self.previous_time = now

        return result
```

Now, we'll run the tests again, and see how we did as follows:

```
python3 -m doctest PIDflawed.txt
```

This immediately tells us that there's a bug in the `calculate_response` method:

```
$ python3 -m doctest PIDflawed.txt
**********************************************************************
File "PIDflawed.txt", line 27, in PIDflawed.txt
Failed example:
    controller.calculate_response(12)
Expected:
    -6.0
Got:
    6.0
**********************************************************************
File "PIDflawed.txt", line 29, in PIDflawed.txt
Failed example:
    controller.calculate_response(6)
Expected:
    -3.0
Got:
    3.0
```

There are more error reports in the same vein. There should be five in total. It seems that the `calculate_response` method is working backwards, producing negatives when it should give us positives, and vice-versa.

We know that we need to look for a sign error in `calculate_response`, and we find it on the fourth line, where the input value should be subtracted from the setpoint and not the other way around. Things should work better if we change this line to the following:

```
err = self.setpoint[-1] - value
```

As expected, that change fixes things. The tests all pass, now.

We used our tests to tell us what was needed to be done, and to tell us when our code was complete. Our first run of the tests gave us a list of things that needed to be written; a to-do list of sorts. After we wrote some code, we ran the tests again to see if it was doing what we expected, which gave us a new to-do list. We kept on alternately running the tests and writing code to make one of the tests pass until they all did. When all the tests pass, either we're done, or we need to write more tests.

Whenever we find a bug that isn't already caught by a test, the right thing to do is to add a test that catches it, and then we need to fix the bug. This gives a fixed bug, but also a test that covers some part of the program that wasn't tested before. Your new test might well catch more bugs that you weren't even aware of, and it will help you avoid recreating the fixed bug.

This "test a little, code a little" style of programming is called **Test-driven Development**, and you'll find that it's very productive.

Notice that the pattern in the way the tests failed was immediately apparent. There's no guarantee that will be the case, of course, but it often is. Combined with the ability to narrow your attention to the specific units that are having problems, debugging is usually a snap.

Feedback

So, we have a PID controller, it passes our tests... are we done? Maybe. Let's ask the client.

The good news is that they mostly like it. They have a few things they'd like to be changed, though. They want us to be able to optionally specify the current time as a parameter to `calculate_response`, so that the specified time is used instead of the current system time. They also want us to change the signature of the constructor so that it accepts an initial measurement and optionally a measurement time as parameters.

So, the program passes all of our tests, but the tests don't correctly describe the requirements anymore. What to do?

First, we'll add the initial value parameter to the constructor tests, and update the expected results as follows:

```
>>> import time
>>> real_time = time.time
>>> time.time = (float(x) for x in range(1, 1000)).__next__
>>> import pid
>>> controller = pid.PID(P = 0.5, I = 0.5, D = 0.5, setpoint = 0,
...                      initial = 12)
>>> controller.gains
(0.5, 0.5, 0.5)
>>> controller.setpoint
[0.0]
>>> controller.previous_time
1.0
>>> controller.previous_error
-12.0
>>> controller.integrated_error
0.0
>>> time.time = real_time
```

Now, we'll add another test of the constructor, a test that checks the correct behavior when the optional initial time parameter is provided:

```
>>> import imp
>>> pid = imp.reload(pid)
>>> controller = pid.PID(P = 0.5, I = 0.5, D = 0.5, setpoint = 1,
...                      initial = 12, when = 43)
>>> controller.gains
(0.5, 0.5, 0.5)
>>> controller.setpoint
[1.0]
>>> controller.previous_time
43.0
>>> controller.previous_error
-11.0
>>> controller.integrated_error
0.0
```

Next, we change the `calculate_response` tests to use the new signature for the constructor:

```
>>> controller = pid.PID(P = 0.5, I = 0.5, D = 0.5, setpoint = 0,
...                      initial = 12)
```

We need to add a second `calculate_response` test that checks whether the function behaves properly when the optional time parameter is passed to it:

```
>>> pid = imp.reload(pid)
>>> controller = pid.PID(P = 0.5, I = 0.5, D = 0.5, setpoint = 0,
...                      initial = 12, when = 1)
>>> controller.calculate_response(6, 2)
-3.0
>>> controller.calculate_response(3, 3)
-4.5
>>> controller.calculate_response(-1.5, 4)
-0.75
>>> controller.calculate_response(-2.25, 5)
-1.125
```

Finally, we adjust the constructor call in the setpoint method tests. This change looks the same as the constructor call changes in the other tests.

When we're adjusting the tests, we discover that the behavior of the `calculate_response` method has changed due to the addition of the initial value and initial time parameters to the constructor. The tests will report this as an error but it's not clear that if it really is wrong, so we check this with the client. After talking it over, the client decides that this is actually correct behavior, so we change our tests to reflect that.

Our complete specification and test document now looks like this (new or changed lines are highlighted):

```
We want a class that implements a PID controller for a single
variable. The measurement, setpoint, and output should all be real
numbers. The constructor should accept an initial measurement value in
addition to the gains and setpoint.

>>> import time
>>> real_time = time.time
>>> time.time = (float(x) for x in range(1, 1000)).__next__
>>> import pid
>>> controller = pid.PID(P = 0.5, I = 0.5, D = 0.5, setpoint = 0,
...                      initial = 12)
>>> controller.gains
(0.5, 0.5, 0.5)
>>> controller.setpoint
[0.0]
>>> controller.previous_time
1.0
>>> controller.previous_error
-12.0
>>> controller.integrated_error
0.0
>>> time.time = real_time

The constructor should also optionally accept a parameter specifying
when the initial measurement was taken.

>>> import imp
>>> pid = imp.reload(pid)
>>> controller = pid.PID(P = 0.5, I = 0.5, D = 0.5, setpoint = 1,
...                      initial = 12, when = 43)
>>> controller.gains
(0.5, 0.5, 0.5)
>>> controller.setpoint
[1.0]
>>> controller.previous_time
```

```
43.0
>>> controller.previous_error
-11.0
>>> controller.integrated_error
0.0

The calculate response method receives the measured value as input,
and returns the control signal.

>>> import time
>>> real_time = time.time
>>> time.time = (float(x) for x in range(1, 1000)).__next__
>>> pid = imp.reload(pid)
>>> controller = pid.PID(P = 0.5, I = 0.5, D = 0.5, setpoint = 0,
...                       initial = 12)
>>> controller.calculate_response(6)
-3.0
>>> controller.calculate_response(3)
-4.5
>>> controller.calculate_response(-1.5)
-0.75
>>> controller.calculate_response(-2.25)
-1.125
>>> time.time = real_time

The calculate_response method should be willing to accept a parameter
specifying at what time the call is happening.

>>> pid = imp.reload(pid)
>>> controller = pid.PID(P = 0.5, I = 0.5, D = 0.5, setpoint = 0,
...                       initial = 12, when = 1)
>>> controller.calculate_response(6, 2)
-3.0
>>> controller.calculate_response(3, 3)
-4.5
>>> controller.calculate_response(-1.5, 4)
-0.75
>>> controller.calculate_response(-2.25, 5)
-1.125

We need to be able to adjust the setpoint at runtime, but we want it
to have a memory, so that we can easily return to the previous
setpoint.
```

```
>>> pid = imp.reload(pid)
>>> controller = pid.PID(P = 0.5, I = 0.5, D = 0.5, setpoint = 0,
...                      initial = 12)
>>> controller.push_setpoint(7)
>>> controller.setpoint
[0.0, 7.0]
>>> controller.push_setpoint(8.5)
>>> controller.setpoint
[0.0, 7.0, 8.5]
>>> controller.pop_setpoint()
8.5
>>> controller.setpoint
[0.0, 7.0]
>>> controller.pop_setpoint()
7.0
>>> controller.setpoint
[0.0]
>>> controller.pop_setpoint()
Traceback (most recent call last):
ValueError: PID controller must have a setpoint
```

Our tests didn't match the requirements and so we needed to change them. That's fine, but we don't want to change them too much because the tests we have already help us to avoid some problems that we've previously spotted or had to fix. The last thing we want for the computer is to stop checking for known problems. Because of this, we very much prefer adding new tests, instead of changing old ones.

This is one reason why we added new tests to check the behavior when the optional time parameters were supplied. The other reason is that, if we added these parameters to the existing tests, we wouldn't have any tests of what happens when you don't use these parameters. We always want to check every code path through each unit.

The addition of the initial parameter to the constructor is a big deal. It not only changes the way the constructor should behave, it also changes the way the `calculate_response` method should behave in a rather dramatic way. Since there is a change in the correct behavior (a fact that we didn't realize until the tests pointed it out to us, which in turn allowed us to get a confirmation of what the correct behavior should be from our clients before we started writing the code), we have no choice but to go through and change the tests, recalculating the expected outputs and all. Doing all that work has a benefit, though, over and above the future ability to check whether the function is working correctly: this makes it much easier to comprehend how the function should work when we actually write it.

When we change a test to reflect new correct behavior, we still try to change it as little as possible. After all, we don't want the test to stop checking for old behavior that's still correct, and we don't want to introduce a bug in the test itself.

> To a certain extent, the code being tested acts as a test of the test, so even bugs in your tests don't survive very long when you use good testing discipline.

Development, again

Time to do some more coding. In real life, we might cycle between development and feedback any number of times, depending on how well we're able to communicate with our clients. In fact, it might be a good thing to increase the number of times we go back and forth, even if this means that each cycle is short. Keeping the clients in the loop and up-to-date is a good thing.

The first step, as always, is to run the tests and get an updated list of the things that need to be done:

```
Python3 -m doctest PID.txt
```

```
$ python3 -m doctest PID.txt
**********************************************************************
File "PID.txt", line 10, in PID.txt
Failed example:
    controller = pid.PID(P = 0.5, I = 0.5, D = 0.5, setpoint = 0,
                         initial = 12)
Exception raised:
    Traceback (most recent call last):
      File "/usr/lib64/python3.3/doctest.py", line 1313, in __run
        compileflags, 1), test.globs)
      File "<doctest PID.txt[4]>", line 2, in <module>
        initial = 12)
    TypeError: __init__() got an unexpected keyword argument 'initial'
**********************************************************************
File "PID.txt", line 12, in PID.txt
Failed example:
    controller.gains
Exception raised:
    Traceback (most recent call last):
      File "/usr/lib64/python3.3/doctest.py", line 1313, in __run
        compileflags, 1), test.globs)
      File "<doctest PID.txt[5]>", line 1, in <module>
        controller.gains
    NameError: name 'controller' is not defined
```

There are actually a lot more errors that are reported, but the very first one gives us a good hint about what we need to fix right off. The constructor needs to change to match the tests' expectations.

Using the `doctest` error report to guide us, and rerunning the tests frequently, we can quickly get our PID class into shape. In practice, this works best using short development cycles where you make only a few changes to the code, and then run the tests again. Fix one thing, and then test again.

Once we've gone back and forth between coding and testing enough times, we'll end up with something like this:

```
from time import time

class PID:
    def __init__(self, P, I, D, setpoint, initial, when = None):
        self.gains = (float(P), float(I), float(D))

        if P < 0 or I < 0 or D < 0:
            raise ValueError('PID controller gains must be non-
negative')

        if not isinstance(setpoint, complex):
            setpoint = float(setpoint)

        if not isinstance(initial, complex):
            initial = float(initial)

        self.setpoint = [setpoint]

        if when is None:
            self.previous_time = time()
        else:
            self.previous_time = float(when)

        self.previous_error = self.setpoint[-1] - initial
        self.integrated_error = 0.0

    def push_setpoint(self, target):
        self.setpoint.append(float(target))

    def pop_setpoint(self):
        if len(self.setpoint) > 1:
            return self.setpoint.pop()
        raise ValueError('PID controller must have a setpoint')
```

```
    def calculate_response(self, value, now = None):
        if now is None:
            now = time()
        else:
            now = float(now)

        P, I, D = self.gains

        err = self.setpoint[-1] - value

        result = P * err
        delta = now - self.previous_time
        self.integrated_error += err * delta
        result += I * self.integrated_error
        result += D * (err - self.previous_error) / delta

        self.previous_error = err
        self.previous_time = now

        return result
```

Once again, all of the tests pass including all of the revised tests from the client, and it's remarkable how rewarding that lack of an error report can be. We're ready to see whether the client is willing to accept delivery of the code yet.

Later stages of the process

There are later phases of development when it's your job to maintain the code, or to integrate it into another product. Functionally, they work in the same way as the development phase. If you're handling pre-existing code and are asked to maintain or integrate it, you'll be much happier if it comes to you with a test suite already written because, until you've mastered the intricacies of the code, the test suite is the only way in which you'll be able to modify the code with confidence.

If you're unfortunate enough to be handed a pile of code with no tests, writing tests is a good first step. Each test you write is one more unit of the code that you can honestly say you understand, and know what to expect from. And, of course, each test you write is one more unit that you can count on to tell you if you introduce a bug.

Summary

We've walked through the process of developing a project using unit testing and test-driven development, paying attention to the ways that we can identify units, and covering some of the ways in which we can isolate `doctest` tests for individual units.

We've also talked about the philosophy and discipline of unit testing, what it is in detail, and why it is valuable.

In the next chapter, we'll discuss mock objects, a powerful tool for isolating units.

4

Decoupling Units with unittest.mock

Several times in the last couple of chapters, when faced with the problem of isolating tests from each other, I told you to just keep the problem in mind and said we'd deal with it in this chapter. Finally, it's time to actually address the problem.

Functions and methods that do not rely on the behavior of other functions, methods, or data are rare; the common case is to have them make several calls to other functions or methods, and instantiate at least one instance of a class. Every one of these calls and instantiations breaks the unit's isolation; or, if you prefer to think of it this way, it incorporates more code into the isolated section.

No matter how you look at it—as an isolation breaking or as expanding the isolated section—it's something you want to have the ability to prevent. Mock objects let you do this by taking the place of external functions or objects.

Using the `unittest.mock` package, you can easily perform the following:

- Replace functions and objects in your own code or in external packages, as we did with `time.time` in *Chapter 3, Unit Testing with doctest*.
- Control how replacement objects behave. You can control what return values they provide, whether they raise an exception, even whether they make any calls to other functions, or create instances of other objects.
- Check whether the replacement objects were used as you expected: whether functions or methods were called the correct number of times, whether the calls occurred in the correct order, and whether the passed parameters were correct.

Mock objects in general

All right, before we get down to the nuts and bolts of `unittest.mock`, let's spend a few moments talking about mock objects overall.

Broadly speaking, mock objects are any objects that you can use as substitutes in your test code, to keep your tests from overlapping and your tested code from infiltrating the wrong tests. Thus, our fake `time.time` from *Chapter 3, Unit Testing with doctest*, was a mock object. However, like most things in programming, the idea works better when it has been formalized into a well-designed library that you can call on when you need it. There are many such libraries available for most programming languages.

Over time, the authors of mock object libraries have developed two major design patterns for mock objects: in one pattern, you can create a mock object and perform all of the expected operations on it. The object records these operations, and then you put the object into playback mode and pass it to your code. If your code fails to duplicate the expected operations, the mock object reports a failure.

In the second pattern, you can create a mock object, do the minimal necessary configuration to allow it to mimic the real object it replaces, and pass it to your code. It records how the code uses it, and then you can perform assertions after the fact to check whether your code used the object as expected.

The second pattern is *slightly* more capable in terms of the tests that you can write using it but, overall, either pattern works well.

Mock objects according to unittest.mock

Python has several mock object libraries; as of Python 3.3, however, one of them has been crowned as a member of the standard library. Naturally that's the one we're going to focus on. That library is, of course, `unittest.mock`.

The `unittest.mock` library is of the second sort, a record-actual-use-and-then-assert library. The library contains several different kinds of mock objects that, between them, let you mock almost anything that exists in Python. Additionally, the library contains several useful helpers that simplify assorted tasks related to mock objects, such as temporarily replacing real objects with mocks.

Standard mock objects

The basic element of `unittest.mock` is the `unittest.mock.Mock` class. Even without being configured at all, `Mock` instances can do a pretty good job of pretending to be some other object, method, or function.

> There are many mock object libraries for Python; so, strictly speaking, the phrase "mock object" could mean any object that was created by any of these libraries. From here on in this book, you can assume that a "mock object" is an instance of `unittest.mock.Mock` or one of its descendants.

Mock objects can pull off this impersonation because of a clever, somewhat recursive trick. When you access an unknown attribute of a mock object, instead of raising an `AttributeError` exception, the mock object creates a child mock object and returns that. Since mock objects are pretty good at impersonating other objects, returning a mock object instead of the real value works at least in the common case.

Similarly, mock objects are callable; when you call a mock object as a function or method, it records the parameters of the call and then, by default, returns a child mock object.

A child mock object is a mock object in its own right, but it knows that it's connected to the mock object it came from—its parent. Anything you do to the child is also recorded in the parent's memory. When the time comes to check whether the mock objects were used correctly, you can use the parent object to check on all of its descendants.

Example: Playing with mock objects in the interactive shell (try it for yourself!):

```
$ python3.4
Python 3.4.0 (default, Apr  2 2014, 08:10:08)
[GCC 4.8.2] on linux
Type "help", "copyright", "credits" or "license" for more information.
>>> from unittest.mock import Mock, call
>>> mock = Mock()
>>> mock.x
<Mock name='mock.x' id='140145643647832'>
>>> mock.x
<Mock name='mock.x' id='140145643647832'>
>>> mock.x('Foo', 3, 14)
<Mock name='mock.x()' id='140145643690640'>
>>> mock.x('Foo', 3, 14)
```

```
<Mock name='mock.x()' id='140145643690640'>
>>> mock.x('Foo', 99, 12)
<Mock name='mock.x()' id='140145643690640'>
>>> mock.y(mock.x('Foo', 1, 1))
<Mock name='mock.y()' id='140145643534320'>
>>> mock.method_calls
[call.x('Foo', 3, 14),
 call.x('Foo', 3, 14),
 call.x('Foo', 99, 12),
 call.x('Foo', 1, 1),
 call.y(<Mock name='mock.x()' id='140145643690640'>)]
>>> mock.assert_has_calls([call.x('Foo', 1, 1)])
>>> mock.assert_has_calls([call.x('Foo', 1, 1), call.x('Foo', 99, 12)])
Traceback (most recent call last):
  File "<stdin>", line 1, in <module>
  File "/usr/lib64/python3.4/unittest/mock.py", line 792, in assert_has_
calls
    ) from cause
AssertionError: Calls not found.
Expected: [call.x('Foo', 1, 1), call.x('Foo', 99, 12)]
Actual: [call.x('Foo', 3, 14),
 call.x('Foo', 3, 14),
 call.x('Foo', 99, 12),
 call.x('Foo', 1, 1),
 call.y(<Mock name='mock.x()' id='140145643690640'>)]
>>> mock.assert_has_calls([call.x('Foo', 1, 1),
...                        call.x('Foo', 99, 12)], any_order = True)
>>> mock.assert_has_calls([call.y(mock.x.return_value)])
>>>
```

There are several important things demonstrated in this interactive session.

First, notice that the *same* mock object was returned each time that we accessed `mock.x`. This always holds true: if you access the same attribute of a mock object, you'll get the same mock object back as the result.

The next thing to notice might seem more surprising. Whenever you call a mock object, you get the same mock object back as the return value. The returned mock isn't made new for every call, nor is it unique for each combination of parameters. We'll see how to override the return value shortly but, by default, you get the same mock object back every time you call a mock object. This mock object can be accessed using the `return_value` attribute name, as you might have noticed from the last statement of the example.

The `unittest.mock` package contains a `call` object that helps to make it easier to check whether the correct calls have been made. The `call` object is callable, and takes note of its parameters in a way similar to mock objects, making it easy to compare it to a mock object's call history. However, the `call` object really shines when you have to check for calls to descendant mock objects. As you can see in the previous example, while `call('Foo', 1, 1)` will match a call to the parent mock object, if the call used these parameters, `call.x('Foo', 1, 1)`, it matches a call to the child mock object named `x`. You can build up a long chain of lookups and invocations. For example:

```
>>> mock.z.hello(23).stuff.howdy('a', 'b', 'c')
<Mock name='mock.z.hello().stuff.howdy()' id='140145643535328'>
>>> mock.assert_has_calls([
...     call.z.hello().stuff.howdy('a', 'b', 'c')
... ])
>>>
```

Notice that the original invocation included `hello(23)`, but the call specification wrote it simply as `hello()`. Each call specification is only concerned with the parameters of the object that was finally called after all of the lookups. The parameters of intermediate calls are not considered. That's okay because they always produce the same return value anyway unless you've overridden that behavior, in which case they probably don't produce a mock object at all.

> You might not have encountered an assertion before. Assertions have one job, and one job only: they raise an exception if something is not as expected. The `assert_has_calls` method, in particular, raises an exception if the mock object's history does not include the specified calls. In our example, the call history matches, so the assertion method doesn't do anything visible.

You *can* check whether the intermediate calls were made with the correct parameters, though, because the mock object recorded a call immediately to `mock.z.hello(23)` before it recorded a call to `mock.z.hello().stuff.howdy('a', 'b', 'c')`:

```
>>> mock.mock_calls.index(call.z.hello(23))
6
>>> mock.mock_calls.index(call.z.hello().stuff.howdy('a', 'b', 'c'))
7
```

This also points out the `mock_calls` attribute that all mock objects carry. If the various assertion functions don't quite do the trick for you, you can always write your own functions that inspect the `mock_calls` list and check whether things are or are not as they should be. We'll discuss the mock object assertion methods shortly.

Non-mock attributes

What if you want a mock object to give back something other than a child mock object when you look up an attribute? It's easy; just assign a value to that attribute:

```
>>> mock.q = 5
>>> mock.q
5
```

There's one other common case where mock objects' default behavior is wrong: what if accessing a particular attribute is supposed to raise an `AttributeError`? Fortunately, that's easy too:

```
>>> del mock.w
>>> mock.w
Traceback (most recent call last):
  File "<stdin>", line 1, in <module>
  File "/usr/lib64/python3.4/unittest/mock.py", line 563, in __getattr__
    raise AttributeError(name)
AttributeError: w
```

Non-mock return values and raising exceptions

Sometimes, actually fairly often, you'll want mock objects posing as functions or methods to return a specific value, or a series of specific values, rather than returning another mock object.

To make a mock object always return the same value, just change the `return_value` attribute:

```
>>> mock.o.return_value = 'Hi'
>>> mock.o()
'Hi'
>>> mock.o('Howdy')
'Hi'
```

If you want the mock object to return different value each time it's called, you need to assign an iterable of return values to the `side_effect` attribute instead, as follows:

```
>>> mock.p.side_effect = [1, 2, 3]
>>> mock.p()
1
>>> mock.p()
2
>>> mock.p()
3
>>> mock.p()
Traceback (most recent call last):
  File "<stdin>", line 1, in <module>
  File "/usr/lib64/python3.4/unittest/mock.py", line 885, in __call__
    return _mock_self._mock_call(*args, **kwargs)
  File "/usr/lib64/python3.4/unittest/mock.py", line 944, in _mock_call
    result = next(effect)
StopIteration
```

If you don't want your mock object to raise a `StopIteration` exception, you need to make sure to give it enough return values for all of the invocations in your test. If you don't know how many times it will be invoked, an infinite iterator such as `itertools.count` might be what you need. This is easily done:

```
>>> mock.p.side_effect = itertools.count()
```

If you want your mock to raise an exception instead of returning a value, just assign the exception object to `side_effect`, or put it into the iterable that you assign to `side_effect`:

```
>>> mock.e.side_effect = [1, ValueError('x')]
>>> mock.e()
1
>>> mock.e()
Traceback (most recent call last):
  File "<stdin>", line 1, in <module>
  File "/usr/lib64/python3.4/unittest/mock.py", line 885, in __call__
    return _mock_self._mock_call(*args, **kwargs)
  File "/usr/lib64/python3.4/unittest/mock.py", line 946, in _mock_call
    raise result
ValueError: x
```

The `side_effect` attribute has another use, as well that we'll talk about.

Mocking class or function details

Sometimes, the generic behavior of mock objects isn't a close enough emulation of the object being replaced. This is particularly the case when it's important that they raise exceptions when used improperly, since mock objects are usually happy to accept any usage.

The `unittest.mock` package addresses this problem using a technique called **speccing**. If you pass an object into `unittest.mock.create_autospec`, the returned value will be a mock object, but it will do its best to pretend that it's the same object you passed into `create_autospec`. This means that it will:

- Raise an `AttributeError` if you attempt to access an attribute that the original object doesn't have, unless you first explicitly assign a value to that attribute
- Raise a `TypeError` if you attempt to call the mock object when the original object wasn't callable
- Raise a `TypeError` if you pass the wrong number of parameters or pass a keyword parameter that isn't viable if the original object was callable
- Trick `isinstance` into thinking that the mock object is of the original object's type

Mock objects made by create_autospec share this trait with all of their children as well, which is usually what you want. If you really just want a specific mock to be specced, while its children are not, you can pass the template object into the Mock constructor using the spec keyword.

Here's a short demonstration of using create_autospec:

```
>>> from unittest.mock import create_autospec
>>> x = Exception('Bad', 'Wolf')
>>> y = create_autospec(x)
>>> isinstance(y, Exception)
True
>>> y
<NonCallableMagicMock spec='Exception' id='140440961099088'>
```

Mocking function or method side effects

Sometimes, for a mock object to successfully take the place of a function or method means that the mock object has to actually perform calls to other functions, or set variable values, or generally do whatever a function can do.

This need is less common than you might think, and it's also somewhat dangerous for testing purposes because, when your mock objects can execute arbitrary code, there's a possibility that they stop being a simplifying tool for enforcing test isolation, and become a complex part of the problem instead.

Having said that, there are still times when you need a mocked function to do something more complex than simply returning a value, and we can use the side_effect attribute of mock objects to achieve this. We've seen side_effect before, when we assigned an iterable of return values to it.

If you assign a callable to side_effect, this callable will be called when the mock object is called and passed the same parameters. If the side_effect function raises an exception, this is what the mock object does as well; otherwise, the side_effect return value is returned by the mock object.

In other words, if you assign a function to a mock object's side_effect attribute, this mock object in effect becomes that function with the only important difference being that the mock object still records the details of how it's used.

The code in a side_effect function should be minimal, and should not try to actually do the job of the code the mock object is replacing. All it should do is perform any expected externally visible operations and then return the expected result.Mock object assertion methods

As we saw in the *Standard mock objects* section, you can always write code that checks the `mock_calls` attribute of mock objects to see whether or not things are behaving as they should. However, there are some particularly common checks that have already been written for you, and are available as assertion methods of the mock objects themselves. As is normal for assertions, these assertion methods return `None` if they pass, and raise an `AssertionError` if they fail.

The `assert_called_with` method accepts an arbitrary collection of arguments and keyword arguments, and raises an `AssertionError` unless these parameters were passed to the mock the last time it was called.

The `assert_called_once_with` method behaves like `assert_called_with`, except that it also checks whether the mock was only called once and raises `AssertionError` if that is not true.

The `assert_any_call` method accepts arbitrary arguments and keyword arguments, and raises an `AssertionError` if the mock object has never been called with these parameters.

We've already seen the `assert_has_calls` method. This method accepts a list of call objects, checks whether they appear in the history in the same order, and raises an exception if they do not. Note that "in the same order" does not necessarily mean "next to each other." There can be other calls in between the listed calls as long as all of the listed calls appear in the proper sequence. This behavior changes if you assign a true value to the `any_order` argument. In that case, `assert_has_calls` doesn't care about the order of the calls, and only checks whether they all appear in the history.

The `assert_not_called` method raises an exception if the mock has ever been called.

Mocking containers and objects with a special behavior

One thing the `Mock` class does not handle is the so-called magic methods that underlie Python's special syntactic constructions: `__getitem__`, `__add__`, and so on. If you need your mock objects to record and respond to magic methods—in other words, if you want them to pretend to be container objects such as dictionaries or lists, or respond to mathematical operators, or act as context managers or any of the other things where syntactic sugar translates it into a method call underneath—you're going to use `unittest.mock.MagicMock` to create your mock objects.

There are a few magic methods that are not supported even by `MagicMock`, due to details of how they (and mock objects) work: `__getattr__`, `__setattr__`, `__init__`, `__new__`, `__prepare__`, `__instancecheck__`, `__subclasscheck__`, and `__del__`.

Here's a simple example in which we use `MagicMock` to create a mock object supporting the `in` operator:

```
>>> from unittest.mock import MagicMock
>>> mock = MagicMock()
>>> 7 in mock
False
>>> mock.mock_calls
[call.__contains__(7)]
>>> mock.__contains__.return_value = True
>>> 8 in mock
True
>>> mock.mock_calls
[call.__contains__(7), call.__contains__(8)]
```

Things work similarly with the other magic methods. For example, addition:

```
>>> mock + 5
<MagicMock name='mock.__add__()' id='140017311217816'>
>>> mock.mock_calls
[call.__contains__(7), call.__contains__(8), call.__add__(5)]
```

Notice that the return value of the addition is a mock object, a child of the original mock object, but the `in` operator returned a Boolean value. Python ensures that some magic methods return a value of a particular type, and will raise an exception if that requirement is not fulfilled. In these cases, `MagicMock's` implementations of the methods return a best-guess value of the proper type, instead of a child mock object.

There's something you need to be careful of when it comes to the in-place mathematical operators, such as `+=` (`__iadd__`) and `|=` (`__ior__`), and that is the fact that `MagicMock` handles them somewhat strangely. What it does is still useful, but it might well catch you by surprise:

```
>>> mock += 10
>>> mock.mock_calls
[]
```

What was that? Did it erase our call history? Fortunately, no, it didn't. What it did was assign the child mock created by the addition operation to the variable called mock. That is entirely in accordance with how the in-place math operators are supposed to work. Unfortunately, it has still cost us our ability to access the call history, since we no longer have a variable pointing at the parent mock object.

> Make sure that you have the parent mock object set aside in a variable that won't be reassigned, if you're going to be checking in-place math operators. Also, you should make sure that your mocked in-place operators return the result of the operation, even if that just means `return self.return_value`, because otherwise Python will assign `None` to the left-hand variable.

There's another detailed way in which in-place operators work that you should keep in mind:

```
>>> mock = MagicMock()
>>> x = mock
>>> x += 5
>>> x
<MagicMock name='mock.__iadd__()' id='139845830142216'>
>>> x += 10
>>> x
<MagicMock name='mock.__iadd__().__iadd__()' id='139845830154168'>
>>> mock.mock_calls
[call.__iadd__(5), call.__iadd__().__iadd__(10)]
```

Because the result of the operation is assigned to the original variable, a series of in-place math operations builds up a chain of child mock objects. If you think about it, that's the right thing to do, but it is rarely what people expect at first.

Mock objects for properties and descriptors

There's another category of things that basic `Mock` objects don't do a good job of emulating: **descriptors**.

Descriptors are objects that allow you to interfere with the normal variable access mechanism. The most commonly used descriptors are created by Python's property built-in function, which simply allows you to write functions to control getting, setting, and deleting a variable.

To mock a property (or other descriptor), create a `unittest.mock.PropertyMock` instance and assign it to the property name. The only complication is that you can't assign a descriptor to an object instance; you have to assign it to the object's type because descriptors are looked up in the type without first checking the instance.

That's not hard to do with mock objects, fortunately:

```
>>> from unittest.mock import PropertyMock
>>> mock = Mock()
>>> prop = PropertyMock()
>>> type(mock).p = prop
>>> mock.p
<MagicMock name='mock()' id='139845830215328'>
>>> mock.mock_calls
[]
>>> prop.mock_calls
[call()]
>>> mock.p = 6
>>> prop.mock_calls
[call(), call(6)]
```

The thing to be mindful of here is that the property is not a child of the object named mock. Because of this, we have to keep it around in its own variable because otherwise we'd have no way of accessing its history.

The `PropertyMock` objects record variable lookup as a call with no parameters, and variable assignment as a call with the new value as a parameter.

> You can use a `PropertyMock` object if you actually need to record variable accesses in your mock object history. Usually you don't need to do that, but the option exists.

Even though you set a property by assigning it to an attribute of a type, you don't have to worry about having your `PropertyMock` objects bleed over into other tests. Each `Mock` you create has its own type object, even though they all claim to be of the same class:

```
>>> type(Mock()) is type(Mock())
False
```

Thanks to this feature, any changes that you make to a mock object's type object are unique to that specific mock object.

Mocking file objects

It's likely that you'll occasionally need to replace a file object with a mock object. The `unittest.mock` library helps you with this by providing `mock_open`, which is a factory for fake open functions. These functions have the same interface as the real open function, but they return a mock object that's been configured to pretend that it's an open file object.

This sounds more complicated than it is. See for yourself:

```
>>> from unittest.mock import mock_open
>>> open = mock_open(read_data = 'moose')
>>> with open('/fake/file/path.txt', 'r') as f:
...    print(f.read())
...
moose
```

If you pass a string value to the `read_data` parameter, the mock file object that eventually gets created will use that value as the data source when its read methods get called. As of Python 3.4.0, `read_data` only supports string objects, not bytes.

If you don't pass `read_data`, `read` method calls will return an empty string.

The problem with the previous code is that it makes the real open function inaccessible, and leaves a mock object lying around where other tests might stumble over it. Read on to see how to fix these problems.

Replacing real code with mock objects

The `unittest.mock` library gives a very nice tool for temporarily replacing objects with mock objects, and then undoing the change when our test is done. This tool is `unittest.mock.patch`.

There are a lot of different ways in which that patch can be used: it works as a context manager, a function decorator, and a class decorator; additionally, it can create a mock object to use for the replacement or it can use the replacement object that you specify. There are a number of other optional parameters that can further adjust the behavior of the patch.

Basic usage is easy:

```
>>> from unittest.mock import patch, mock_open
>>> with patch('builtins.open', mock_open(read_data = 'moose')) as mock:
...     with open('/fake/file.txt', 'r') as f:
```

```
...         print(f.read())
...
moose
>>> open
<built-in function open>
```

As you can see, `patch` dropped the mock open function created by `mock_open` over the top of the real open function; then, when we left the context, it replaced the original for us automatically.

The first parameter of `patch` is the only one that is required. It is a string describing the absolute path to the object to be replaced. The path can have any number of package and subpackage names, but it must include the module name and the name of the object inside the module that is being replaced. If the path is incorrect, `patch` will raise an `ImportError`, `TypeError`, or `AttributeError`, depending on what exactly is wrong with the path.

If you don't want to worry about making a mock object to be the replacement, you can just leave that parameter off:

```
>>> import io
>>> with patch('io.BytesIO'):
...     x = io.BytesIO(b'ascii data')
...     io.BytesIO.mock_calls
[call(b'ascii data')]
```

The `patch` function creates a new `MagicMock` for you if you don't tell it what to use for the replacement object. This usually works pretty well, but you can pass the new parameter (also the second parameter, as we used it in the first example of this section) to specify that the replacement should be a particular object; or you can pass the `new_callable` parameter to make patch use the value of that parameter to create the replacement object.

We can also force the patch to use `create_autospec` to make the replacement object, by passing `autospec=True`:

```
>>> with patch('io.BytesIO', autospec = True):
...     io.BytesIO.melvin
Traceback (most recent call last):
  File "<stdin>", line 2, in <module>
  File "/usr/lib64/python3.4/unittest/mock.py", line 557, in __getattr__
    raise AttributeError("Mock object has no attribute %r" % name)
AttributeError: Mock object has no attribute 'melvin'
```

The `patch` function will normally refuse to replace an object that does not exist; however, if you pass it `create=True`, it will happily drop a mock object wherever you like. Naturally, this is not compatible with `autospec=True`.

The `patch` function covers the most common cases. There are a few related functions that handle less common but still useful cases.

The `patch.object` function does the same thing as `patch`, except that, instead of taking the path string, it accepts an object and an attribute name as its first two parameters. Sometimes this is more convenient than figuring out the path to an object. Many objects don't even have valid paths (for example, objects that exist only in a function local scope), although the need to patch them is rarer than you might think.

The `patch.dict` function temporarily drops one or more objects into a dictionary under specific keys. The first parameter is the target dictionary; the second is a dictionary from which to get the key and value pairs to put into the target. If you pass `clear=True`, the target will be emptied before the new values are inserted. Notice that `patch.dict` doesn't create the replacement values for you. You'll need to make your own mock objects, if you want them.

Mock objects in action

That was a lot of theory interspersed with unrealistic examples. Let's take a look at what we've learned and apply it to the tests from the previous chapters for a more realistic view of how these tools can help us.

Better PID tests

The PID tests suffered mostly from having to do a lot of extra work to patch and unpatch `time.time`, and had some difficulty breaking the dependence on the constructor.

Patching time.time

Using `patch`, we can remove a lot of the repetitiveness of dealing with `time.time`; this means that it's less likely that we'll make a mistake somewhere, and saves us from spending time on something that's kind of boring and annoying. All of the tests can benefit from similar changes:

```
>>> from unittest.mock import Mock, patch
>>> with patch('time.time', Mock(side_effect = [1.0, 2.0, 3.0, 4.0,
5.0])):
...     import pid
```

```
...     controller = pid.PID(P = 0.5, I = 0.5, D = 0.5, setpoint = 0,
...                          initial = 12)
...     assert controller.gains == (0.5, 0.5, 0.5)
...     assert controller.setpoint == [0.0]
...     assert controller.previous_time == 1.0
...     assert controller.previous_error == -12.0
...     assert controller.integrated_error == 0.0
```

Apart from using `patch` to handle `time.time`, this test has been changed. We can now use `assert` to check whether things are correct instead of having doctest compare the values directly. There's hardly any difference between the two approaches, except that we can place the `assert` statements inside the context managed by `patch`.

Decoupling from the constructor

Using mock objects, we can finally separate the tests for the PID methods from the constructor, so that mistakes in the constructor cannot affect the outcome:

```
>>> with patch('time.time', Mock(side_effect = [2.0, 3.0, 4.0, 5.0])):
...     pid = imp.reload(pid)
...     mock = Mock()
...     mock.gains = (0.5, 0.5, 0.5)
...     mock.setpoint = [0.0]
...     mock.previous_time = 1.0
...     mock.previous_error = -12.0
...     mock.integrated_error = 0.0
...     assert pid.PID.calculate_response(mock, 6) == -3.0
...     assert pid.PID.calculate_response(mock, 3) == -4.5
...     assert pid.PID.calculate_response(mock, -1.5) == -0.75
...     assert pid.PID.calculate_response(mock, -2.25) == -1.125
```

What we've done here is set up a mock object with the proper attributes, and pass it into `calculate_response` as the self-parameter. We could do this because we didn't create a PID instance at all. Instead, we looked up the method's function inside the class and called it directly, allowing us to pass whatever we wanted as the self-parameter instead of having Python's automatic mechanisms handle it.

Never invoking the constructor means that we're immune to any errors it might contain, and guarantees that the object state is exactly what we expect here in our `calculate_response` test.

Summary

In this chapter, we've learned about a family of objects that specialize in impersonating other classes, objects, methods, and functions. We've seen how to configure these objects to handle corner cases where their default behavior isn't sufficient, and we've learned how to examine the activity logs that these mock objects keep, so that we can decide whether the objects are being used properly or not.

In the next chapter, we'll look at Python's `unittest` package, a more structured testing framework that is less useful for communicating with people than `doctest` is, but better able to handle the complexities of large-scale testing.

5
Structured Testing with unittest

The `doctest` tool is flexible and extremely easy to use but, as we've noticed, it falls somewhat short when it comes to writing disciplined tests. That's not to say that it's impossible; we've seen that we can write well-behaved, isolated tests in `doctest`. The problem is that `doctest` doesn't do any of that work for us. Fortunately, we have another testing tool on hand, a tool that requires a bit more structure in our tests, and provides a bit more support: `unittest`.

The `unittest` module was designed based on the requirements of unit testing, but it's not actually limited to that. You can use unit test for integration and system testing, too.

Like `doctest`, `unittest` is a part of the Python standard library; thus, if you've got Python, you have unit test.

In this chapter, we're going to cover the following topics:

- Writing tests within the `unittest` framework
- Running our new tests
- Looking at the features that make `unittest` a good choice for larger test suites

The basics

Before we start talking about new concepts and features, let's take a look at how to use `unittest` to express the ideas that we've already learned about. That way, we'll have something solid on which ground our new understanding.

We're going to revisit the `PID` class, or at least the tests for the `PID` class, from *Chapter 3, Unit Testing with doctest*. We're going to rewrite the tests so that they operate within the `unittest` framework.

Before moving on, take a moment to refer back to the final version of the `pid.txt` file from *Chapter 3, Unit Testing with doctest*. We'll be implementing the same tests using the `unittest` framework.

Create a new file called `test_pid.py` in the same directory as `pid.py`. Notice that this is a `.py` file: `unittest` tests are pure Python source code, rather than being plain text with source code embedded in it. This means that the tests will be less useful from a documentary point of view, but grants other benefits in exchange.

Insert the following code into your newly created `test_pid.py` file:

```
from unittest import TestCase, main
from unittest.mock import Mock, patch

import pid

class test_pid_constructor(TestCase):
    def test_constructor_with_when_parameter(self):
        controller = pid.PID(P = 0.5, I = 0.5, D = 0.5,
                             setpoint = 1, initial = 12,
                             when = 43)

        self.assertEqual(controller.gains, (0.5, 0.5, 0.5))
        self.assertAlmostEqual(controller.setpoint[0], 1.0)
        self.assertEqual(len(controller.setpoint), 1)
        self.assertAlmostEqual(controller.previous_time, 43.0)
        self.assertAlmostEqual(controller.previous_error, -11.0)
        self.assertAlmostEqual(controller.integrated_error, 0)
```

It has been argued, sometimes with good reason, that unit tests should not contain more than one assertion. The idea is that each unit test should test one thing and one thing only, to further narrow down what the problem is, when the test fails. It's a good point but not something to be overly fanatic about, in my opinion. In cases like the preceding code, splitting each assertion out into its own test function will not produce any more informative error messages than we get in this way; it would just increase our overhead.

My rule of thumb is that a test function can have any number of trivial assertions, and at most one non-trivial assertion:

```
    @patch('pid.time', Mock(side_effect = [1.0]))
    def test_constructor_without_when_parameter(self):
```

```
        controller = pid.PID(P = 0.5, I = 0.5, D = 0.5,
                             setpoint = 0, initial = 12)

        self.assertEqual(controller.gains, (0.5, 0.5, 0.5))
        self.assertAlmostEqual(controller.setpoint[0], 0.0)
        self.assertEqual(len(controller.setpoint), 1)
        self.assertAlmostEqual(controller.previous_time, 1.0)
        self.assertAlmostEqual(controller.previous_error, -12.0)
        self.assertAlmostEqual(controller.integrated_error, 0)

class test_pid_calculate_response(TestCase):
    def test_with_when_parameter(self):
        mock = Mock()
        mock.gains = (0.5, 0.5, 0.5)
        mock.setpoint = [0.0]
        mock.previous_time = 1.0
        mock.previous_error = -12.0
        mock.integrated_error = 0.0

        self.assertEqual(pid.PID.calculate_response(mock, 6, 2), -3)
        self.assertEqual(pid.PID.calculate_response(mock, 3, 3), -4.5)
        self.assertEqual(pid.PID.calculate_response(mock, -1.5, 4),
-0.75)
        self.assertEqual(pid.PID.calculate_response(mock, -2.25, 5),
-1.125)


    @patch('pid.time', Mock(side_effect = [2.0, 3.0, 4.0, 5.0]))
    def test_without_when_parameter(self):
        mock = Mock()
        mock.gains = (0.5, 0.5, 0.5)
        mock.setpoint = [0.0]
        mock.previous_time = 1.0
        mock.previous_error = -12.0
        mock.integrated_error = 0.0

        self.assertEqual(pid.PID.calculate_response(mock, 6), -3)
        self.assertEqual(pid.PID.calculate_response(mock, 3), -4.5)
        self.assertEqual(pid.PID.calculate_response(mock, -1.5),
-0.75)
        self.assertEqual(pid.PID.calculate_response(mock, -2.25),
-1.125)
```

Now, run the tests by typing the following on the command line:

```
python3 -m unittest discover
```

You should see output similar to this:

```
$ python3.4 -m unittest discover
....
----------------------------------------------------------------------
Ran 4 tests in 0.001s

OK
```

So, what did we do there? There are several things to notice:

- First, all of the tests are their own methods of classes that inherit from `unittest.TestCase`.
- The tests are named `test_<something>`, where `<something>` is a description to help you (and others who share the code) remember what the test is actually checking. This matters because `unittest` (and several other testing tools) use the name to differentiate tests from non-test methods. As a rule of thumb, your test method names and test module filenames should start with test.
- Because each test is a method, each test naturally runs in its own variable scope. Right here, we gain a big advantage from keeping the tests isolated.
- We inherited a bunch of `assert<Something>` methods from `TestCase`. These give us more flexible ways of checking whether values match, and provide more useful error reports, than Python's basic `assert` statement.
- We used `unittest.mock.patch` as a method decorator. In *Chapter 4, Decoupling Units with unittest.mock*, we used it as a context manager. Either way, it does the same thing: it replaces an object with a mock object, and then puts the original back. When used as a decorator, the replacement happens before the method runs, and the original is put back after the method is complete. That's exactly what we need when our test is a method, so we'll be doing it in this way quite a lot.
- We didn't patch over `time.time`, we patched `over pid.time`. This is because we're not reimporting the `pid` module for each test here. The `pid` module contains `from time import time`, which means that, when it is first loaded, the `time` function is referenced directly into the `pid` module's scope. From then on, changing `time.time` doesn't have any effect on `pid.time`, unless we change it and then reimport the `pid` module. Instead of going to all that trouble, we just patched `pid.time` directly.

- We didn't tell `unittest` which tests to run. Instead, we told it to discover them and it found the tests on its own and ran them automatically. This often works well and saves effort. We'll be looking at a more elaborate tool for test discovery and execution in *Chapter 6, Running Your Tests with Nose*.
- The `unittest` module prints out one dot for each successful test. It will give you more information for tests that fail, or raise an unexpected exception.

The actual tests we performed are the same ones that were written in `doctest`. So far, all we're seeing is a different way of expressing them.

Each test method embodies a single test of a single unit. This gives us a convenient way to structure our tests, grouping together related tests into the same class so that they're easier to find. You might have noticed that we used two test classes in the example. This was for organizational purposes in this case, although there can also be good practical reasons to separate your tests into multiple classes. We'll talk about that soon.

Putting each test into its own method means that each test executes in an isolated namespace, which makes it easier to keep `unittest`-style tests from interfering with each other, relative to `doctest`-style tests. This also means that `unittest` knows how many unit tests are in your test file, instead of simply knowing how many expressions there are (you might have noticed that `doctest` counts each `>>>` line as a separate test). Finally, putting each test in its own method means that each test has a name, which can be a valuable feature. When you run `unittest`, it will include the names of any failing tests in the error report.

Tests in `unittest` don't directly care about anything that isn't part of a call to one of the `TestCase` `assert` methods. This means that we don't have to be bothered about the return values of any functions we call or the results of any expressions we use, unless they're important to the test. This also means that we need to remember to write an assert describing every aspect of the test that we want to have checked. We'll go through the various assertion methods of `TestCase` shortly.

Assertions

Assertions are the mechanism we use to tell `unittest` what the important outcomes of the test are. By using appropriate assertions, we can tell `unittest` exactly what to expect from each test.

The assertTrue method

When we call `self.assertTrue(expression)`, we're telling `unittest` that the expression must be true in order for the test to be a success.

This is a very flexible assertion, since you can check for nearly anything by writing the appropriate Boolean expression. It's also one of the last assertions you should consider using, because it doesn't tell `unittest` anything about the kind of comparison you're making, which means that `unittest` can't tell you clearly what's gone wrong if the test fails.

For example, consider the following test code containing two tests that are guaranteed to fail:

```
from unittest import TestCase

class two_failing_tests(TestCase):
    def test_one_plus_one_equals_one_is_true(self):
        self.assertTrue(1 == 1 + 1)

    def test_one_plus_one_equals_one(self):
        self.assertEqual(1, 1 + 1)
```

It might seem that the two tests are interchangeable, since they both test the same thing. Certainly they'll both fail (or, in the unlikely event that one equals two, they'll both pass), so why prefer one over the other?

Run the tests and see what happens (and also notice that the tests were not executed in the same order as we wrote them; the tests are totally independent of each other, so that's okay, right?).

Both the tests fail, as expected, but the test that uses `assertEqual` tells us:

```
AssertionError: 1 != 2
```

The other one says:

```
AssertionError: False is not true
```

It's pretty clear which of these outputs is more useful in this situation. The `assertTrue` test was able to correctly determine that the test should fail, but it didn't know enough to report any useful information about why it failed. The `assertEqual` test, on the other hand, knew first of all that it was checking whether the two expressions were equal, and second it knew how to present the results so that they would be most useful: by evaluating each of the expressions that it was comparing and placing a `!=` symbol between the results. It tells us both which expectation failed, and what the relevant expressions evaluate to.

The assertFalse method

The `assertFalse` method will succeed when the `assertTrue` method will fail, and vice versa. It has the same limits in terms of producing useful output that `assertTrue` has, and the same flexibility in terms of being able to test nearly any condition.

The assertEqual method

As mentioned in the `assertTrue` discussion, the `assertEqual` assertion checks whether its two parameters are in fact equal, and reports a failure if they are not, along with the actual values of the parameters.

The assertNotEqual method

The `assertNotEqual` assertion fails whenever the `assertEqual` assertion would have succeeded, and vice versa. When it reports a failure, its output indicates that the values of the two expressions are equal, and provides you with those values.

The assertAlmostEqual method

As we've seen before, comparing floating point numbers can be troublesome. In particular, checking whether two floating point numbers are equal is problematic, because things that you might expect to be equal—things that, mathematically, are equal—may still end up differing down among the least significant bits. Floating point numbers only compare equal when every bit is the same.

To address this problem, `unittest` provides `assertAlmostEqual`, which checks whether the two floating point values are almost the same; a small amount of difference between them is tolerated.

Let's look at this problem in action. If you take the square root of seven, and then square it, the result should be seven. Here's a pair of tests that check this fact:

```
from unittest import TestCase

class floating_point_problems(TestCase):
    def test_square_root_of_seven_squared_incorrectly(self):
        self.assertEqual((7.0 ** 0.5) ** 2.0, 7.0)

    def test_square_root_of_seven_squared(self):
        self.assertAlmostEqual((7.0 ** 0.5) ** 2.0, 7.0)
```

The `test_square_root_of_seven_squared_incorrectly` method checks that $\sqrt{7}^2 = {7^{\frac{1}{2}}}^2 = 7$, which is true in reality. In the more specialized number system available to computers, though, taking the square root of 7 and then squaring it doesn't quite get us back to 7, so this test will fail. We will look more closely at this in a moment.

The `test_square_root_of_seven_squared` method checks $\sqrt{7}^2 = {7^{\frac{1}{2}}}^2 \approx 7$, which even the computer will find to be true, so this test should pass.

Unfortunately, floating point numbers (the representation of real numbers used by computers) are not precise, because the majority of numbers on the real number line cannot be represented with a finite, non-repeating sequence of digits, much less than a mere 64 bits. Consequently, what you get back from evaluating the mathematical expression in the previous example is not quite seven. It's good enough for government work though—or practically any other sort of work as well—so we don't want our test to quibble over that tiny difference. Because of this, we should habitually use `assertAlmostEqual` and `assertNotAlmostEqual` when we're comparing floating point numbers with equality.

> This problem doesn't generally carry over into other comparison operators. Checking whether one floating point number is less than the other, for example, is very unlikely to produce the wrong result due to insignificant errors. It's only in cases of equality that this problem bites us.

The assertNotAlmostEqual method

The `assertNotAlmostEqual` assertion fails whenever the `assertAlmostEqual` assertion would have succeeded, and vice versa. When it reports a failure, its output indicates that the values of the two expressions are nearly equal, and provides you with those values.

The assertIs and assertIsNot methods

The `assertIs` and `assertIsNot` methods have the same relationship with Python's `is` operator that `assertEqual` and `assertNotEqual` have to Python's `==` operator. What this means is that they check whether the two operands are (or are not) exactly the same object.

The assertIsNone and assertIsNotNone methods

The `assertIsNone` and `assertIsNotNone` methods are like `assertIs` and `assertIsNot`, except that they accept only one parameter that they always compare to `None`, rather than accepting two parameters and comparing them to each other.

The assertIn and assertNotIn methods

The `assertIn` method is used for checking container objects such as dictionaries, tuples, lists, and sets. If the first parameter is contained in the second, the assertion passes. If not, the assertion fails. The `assertNotIn` method performs the inverse check.

The assertIsInstance and assertNotIsInstance methods

The `assertIsInstance` method checks whether the object passed as the first parameter is an instance of the class passed as the second parameter. The `assertNotIsInstance` method performs the opposite check, ensuring that the object is not an instance of the class.

The assertRaises method

As always, we need to make sure that our units correctly signal errors. Doing the right thing when they receive good inputs is only half the job; they need to do something reasonable when they receive bad inputs, as well.

The `assertRaises` method checks whether a callable raises a specified exception when passed a specified set of parameters.

> A callable is a function, a method, a class, or an object of any arbitrary type that has a `__call__` method.

This assertion only works with callables, which means that you don't have a way of checking whether other sorts of expressions raise an expected exception. If that doesn't fit the needs of your test, it's possible to construct your own test using the `fail` method, described below.

To use `assertRaises`, first pass the expected exception to it, then the callable, and then the parameters that should be passed to the callable when it's invoked.

Here's an example test using `assertRaises`. This test ought to fail, because the callable won't raise the expected exception. `'8ca2'` is a perfectly acceptable input to `int`, when you're also passing `base = 16` to it. Notice that `assertRaises` will accept any number of positional or keyword arguments, and pass them on to the callable on invocation:

```
from unittest import TestCase

class silly_int_test(TestCase):
    def test_int_from_string(self):
        self.assertRaises(ValueError, int, '8ca2', base = 16)
```

When we run this test, it fails (as we knew it would) because `int` didn't raise the exception we told `assertRaises` to expect. The test fails and reports this as follows:

```
AssertionError: ValueError not raised by int
```

If an exception is raised, but it's not the one you told `unittest` to expect, then `unittest` considers that as an error. An error is different from a failure. A failure means that one of your tests has detected a problem in the unit being tested. An error means that there's a problem with the test itself.

The fail method

When all else fails, you can fall back on `fail`. When the code in your test calls fail, the test fails.

What good does that do? When none of the `assert` methods do what you need, you can instead write your checks in such a way that `fail` will be called if the test does not pass. This allows you to use the full expressiveness of Python to describe checks for your expectations.

Let's take a look at an example. This time, we're going to test on a less-than operation, which isn't one of the operations directly supported by an `assert` method. Using fail, it's easy to implement the test anyhow:

```
from unittest import TestCase

class test_with_fail(TestCase):
    def test_less_than(self):
        if not (2.3 < 5.6):
            self.fail('2.3 is not less than 5.6, but it should be')
```

> If a particular comparison gets used repeatedly in your tests, you can write your own `assert` function for that comparison, using `fail` to report errors just as we did in the preceding example.

A couple of things to notice here. First of all, take note of the `not` in the `if` statement. Since we want to run `fail` if the test should *not* pass, but we're used to describing the circumstances when the test should succeed, a good way to write the test is to write the success condition, and then invert it with `not`. That way we can continue thinking in the way we're used to when we use `fail`. The second thing to note is that you can pass a message to fail when you call it; it will be printed out in `unittest` report of failed tests. If you choose your message carefully, it can be a big help.

Make sure you get it

Take a look at the following `doctest`. Can you work out how the equivalent `unittest` would look like?

```
>>> try:
...     int('123')
... except ValueError:
...     pass
... else:
...     print('Expected exception was not raised')
```

That `doctest` code tries to convert a string into an integer; if this conversion does not raise a `ValueError`, it reports an error. In `unittest`, that looks like this:

```
class test_exceptions(TestCase):
    def test_ValueError(self):
        self.assertRaises(ValueError, int, '123')
```

How do you check whether two floating point numbers are equal in `unittest`? You should use the `assertAlmostEqual` method, so as not to get tripped by the floating point imprecision.

When would you choose to use `assertTrue`? How about `fail`? You would use `assertTrue` if none of the more specialized assertions suit your needs. You would use fail if you need maximum control when a test succeeds or fails.

Look back at some of the tests we wrote in the previous chapters, and translate them from `doctest` into `unittest`. Given what you already know of `unittest`, you should be able to translate any of the tests.

While you're doing this, think about the relative merits of `unittest` and `doctest` for each of the tests that you translate. The two systems have different strengths, so it makes sense that each will be the more appropriate choice for different situations. When is `doctest` the better choice, and when is `unittest`?

Test fixtures

The `unittest` has an important and highly useful capability that `doctest` lacks. You can tell `unittest` how to create a standardized environment for your unit tests to run inside, and how to clean up that environment when it's done. This ability to create and later destroy a standardized test environment is a test fixture. While test fixtures don't actually make any tests possible that were impossible before, they can certainly make them shorter and less repetitive.

Example – testing database-backed units

Many programs need to access a database for their operation, which means that many of the units these programs are made of also access a database. The point is that the purpose of a database is to store information and make it accessible in other, arbitrary places; in other words, databases exist to break the isolation of units. The same problem applies to other information stores as well: for example, files in permanent storage.

How do we deal with that? After all, just leaving the units that interact with the database untested is no solution. We need to create an environment where the database connection works as usual, but where any changes that are made do not last. There are a few different ways in which we can do this but, no matter what the details are, we need to set up the special database connection before each test that uses it, and we need to destroy any changes after each such test.

The `unittest` helps us do this by providing test fixtures via the `setUp` and `tearDown` methods of the `TestCase` class. These methods exist for us to override, with the default versions doing nothing.

Here's some database-using code (let's say it exists in a file called `employees.py`), for which we're going to write tests:

```
class Employees:
    def __init__(self, connection):
        self.connection = connection

    def add_employee(self, first, last, date_of_employment):
        cursor = self.connection.cursor()
        cursor.execute('''insert into employees
```

```
                                (first, last, date_of_employment)
                              values
                                (:first, :last, :date_of_employment)''',
                           locals())
            self.connection.commit()

            return cursor.lastrowid

        def find_employees_by_name(self, first, last):
            cursor = self.connection.cursor()
            cursor.execute('''select * from employees
                              where
                                first like :first
                              and
                                last like :last''',
                           locals())

            for row in cursor:
                yield row

        def find_employees_by_date(self, date):
            cursor = self.connection.cursor()
            cursor.execute('''select * from employees
                              where date_of_employment = :date''',
                           locals())

            for row in cursor:
                yield row
```

> The preceding code uses the sqlite3 database that ships with Python. Since the `sqlite3` interface is compatible with Python's DB-API 2.0, any database backend you find yourself using will have a similar interface to what you see here.

We'll start off by importing the needed modules and introducing our `TestCase` subclass:

```
from unittest import TestCase
from sqlite3 import connect, PARSE_DECLTYPES
from datetime import date
from employees import Employees

class test_employees(TestCase):
```

We need a `setUp` method to create the environment that our tests depend on. In this case, that means creating a new database connection to an in-memory-only database, and populating that database with the needed tables and rows:

```
    def setUp(self):
        connection = connect(':memory:',
                             detect_types = PARSE_DECLTYPES)
        cursor = connection.cursor()

        cursor.execute('''create table employees
                            (first text,
                             last text,
                             date_of_employment date)''')

        cursor.execute('''insert into employees
                            (first, last, date_of_employment)
                          values
                            ("Test1", "Employee", :date)''',
                       {'date': date(year = 2003,
                                     month = 7,
                                     day = 12)})

        cursor.execute('''insert into employees
                            (first, last, date_of_employment)
                          values
                            ("Test2", "Employee", :date)''',
                       {'date': date(year = 2001,
                                     month = 3,
                                     day = 18)})

        self.connection = connection
```

We need a `tearDown` method to undo whatever the `setUp` method did, so that each test can run in an untouched version of the environment. Since the database is only in memory, all we have to do is close the connection, and it goes away. The `tearDown` method may end up being much more complicated in other scenarios:

```
    def tearDown(self):
        self.connection.close()
```

Finally, we need the tests themselves:

```
    def test_add_employee(self):
        to_test = Employees(self.connection)
        to_test.add_employee('Test1', 'Employee', date.today())
```

```
        cursor = self.connection.cursor()
        cursor.execute('''select * from employees
                          order by date_of_employment''')

        self.assertEqual(tuple(cursor),
                         (('Test2', 'Employee', date(year = 2001,
                                                     month = 3,
                                                     day = 18)),
                          ('Test1', 'Employee', date(year = 2003,
                                                     month = 7,
                                                     day = 12)),
                          ('Test1', 'Employee', date.today())))

    def test_find_employees_by_name(self):
        to_test = Employees(self.connection)

        found = tuple(to_test.find_employees_by_name('Test1',
'Employee'))
        expected = (('Test1', 'Employee', date(year = 2003,
                                               month = 7,
                                               day = 12)),)

        self.assertEqual(found, expected)

    def test_find_employee_by_date(self):
        to_test = Employees(self.connection)

        target = date(year = 2001, month = 3, day = 18)
        found = tuple(to_test.find_employees_by_date(target))

        expected = (('Test2', 'Employee', target),)

        self.assertEqual(found, expected)
```

We just used a `setUp` method in our `TestCase`, along with a matching `tearDown` method. Between them, these methods made sure that the environment in which the tests were executed was the one they needed (that was `setUp`'s job) and that the environment of each test was cleaned up after the test was run, so that the tests didn't interfere with each other (this was the job of `tearDown`). The `unittest` made sure that `setUp` was run once before each test method, and that `tearDown` was run once after each test method.

Because a test fixture—as defined by `setUp` and `tearDown`—gets wrapped around every test in a `TestCase` class, the `setUp` and `tearDown` methods for the `TestCase` classes that contain too many tests can get very complicated and waste a lot of time dealing with details that are unnecessary for some of the tests. You can avoid this problem by simply grouping together those tests that require specific aspects of the environment into their own `TestCase` classes. Give each `TestCase` an appropriate `setUp` and `tearDown`, only dealing with those aspects of the environment that are necessary for the tests it contains. You can have as many `TestCase` classes as you want, so there's no need to skimp on them when you're deciding which tests to group together.

Notice how simple the `tearDown` method we used was. That's usually a good sign: when the changes that need to be undone in the `tearDown` method are simple to describe, it often means that you can be sure of doing this perfectly. Since any imperfection of the `tearDown` method makes it possible for the tests to leave behind stray data that might alter how other tests behave, getting it right is important. In this case, all of our changes were confined inside the database, so getting rid of the database does the trick.

We could have used a mock object for the database connection, instead. There's nothing wrong with that approach, except that, in this case, it would have been more effort for us. Sometimes mock objects are the perfect tool for the job, sometimes test fixtures save effort; sometimes you need both to get the job done easily.

Summary

This chapter contained a lot of information about how to use the `unittest` framework to write your tests.

Specifically, we covered how to use `unittest` to express concepts you were already familiar with from `doctest`; differences and similarities between `unittest` and doctest; how to use test fixtures to embed your tests in a controlled and temporary environment; and how to use the `unittest.mock` patch to decorate test methods to further control the environment the test executes inside.

In the next chapter, we'll look at a tool called Nose that is capable of finding and running `doctest` tests, `unittest` tests, and ad hoc tests all in the same test run and of providing you with a unified test report.

6
Running Your Tests with Nose

In the last chapter, we saw the `unittest` discover tool find our tests without being told explicitly where they were. That was pretty handy, compared to the way `doctest` had been making us tell it exactly where to find the tests it should run, particularly, when we're talking about a large source tree that has tests in many locations.

Nose is a tool that expands on this idea. It's capable of finding `unittest` tests, `doctest` tests, and ad hoc tests throughout a source tree, and running them all. It then presents you with a unified report of test successes and failures. In other words, Nose lets you pick the right testing tool for any given test, integrating them simply and conveniently.

Nose also provides a few new testing features, such as module-level fixtures and some new assert functions.

Installing Nose

Nose is not a part of the Python standard library, which means that you'll need to install it yourself. You can install Nose with a single command:

```
python3 -m pip install --user nose
```

> If the command reports that no module named `pip` was found, you need to run the following command to install the `pip` module:
>
> **`python3 -m ensurepip --user`**
>
> The `ensurepip` module is part of the standard library as of Python 3.4, so you can count on it being available. You probably won't need this, though, because, even though `pip` isn't part of the standard library, it is bundled with Python releases.

The `--user` command-line switch in the previous command tells the tool to install into your personal Python package folder. If you leave that out of the command, it will try to install Nose for all users.

That's it. Nose is ready to go.

Organizing tests

All right, we've got Nose installed, so what's it good for? Nose looks through a directory structure, finds the test files, sorts out the tests that they contain, runs the tests, and reports the results back to you. That's a lot of work that you don't have to do each time you want to run your tests—which should be often.

Nose recognizes the test files based on their names. Any file or directory whose name contains `test` or `Test` either at the beginning or following any of the characters _ (underscore), . (dot), or - (dash) is recognized as a place where the tests might be found. So are Python source files and package directories. Any file that might contain tests is checked for `unittest TestCases` as well as any functions whose names indicate that they're tests. Nose can find and execute the `doctest` tests, as well, that are either embedded in docstrings or written in separate test files. By default, it won't look for the `doctest` tests unless we tell it to. We'll see how to change the default settings shortly.

Since Nose is so willing to go looking for our tests, we have a lot of freedom with respect to how we can organize them. It often turns out to be a good idea to separate all of the tests into their own directory, or larger projects into a whole tree of directories. A big project can end up having many thousands of tests, so organizing them for easy navigation is a big benefit. If doctests are being used as documentation as well as testing, it's probably a good idea to store them in yet another separate directory with a name that communicates that they are documentary. For a moderately-sized project, this recommended structure might look like the following:

```
Project
  |
  |-- package
  |     |-- __init__.py
  |     |-- module1.py
  |     |-- module2.py
  |     |-- ...
  |
  |-- tests
  |     |-- test_module1.py
  |     |-- test_module2.py
  |     |-- ...
  |
  |-- docs_with_tests
        |-- module1.txt
        |-- module2.txt
        |-- ...
```

This structure is only a recommendation... it's for your benefit, not for Nose. If you feel that a different structure will make things easier for you, go ahead and use it.

An example of organizing tests

We're going to take some of our tests from the previous chapters and organize them into a tree of directories. Then, we're going to use Nose to run them all.

The first step is to create a directory that will hold our code and tests. You can call it whatever you like, but I'll refer to is as `project` here.

Copy the `pid.py`, `avl_tree.py`, and `employees.py` files from the previous chapters into the `project` directory. Also place `test.py` from *Chapter 2, Working with doctest*, here, but rename it to `inline_doctest.py`. We want it to be treated as a source file, not as a test file, so you can see how Nose handles source files with doctests in their docstrings. Modules and packages placed in the `project` directory will be available for tests no matter where the test is placed in the tree.

Create a subdirectory of `project` called `test_chapter2`, and place the `AVL.txt` and `test.txt` files from *Chapter 2, Working with doctest*, into it.

Create a subdirectory of `project` called `test_chapter3`, and place `PID.txt` into it.

Create a subdirectory of `project` called `test_chapter5`, and place all of the `test_*` modules from *Chapter 5, Structured Testing with unittest*, into it.

Now, we're ready to run our tests using the following code:

```
python3 -m nose --with-doctest --doctest-extension=txt -v
```

> You can leave off the `-v` if you want. It just tells Nose to provide a more detailed report.

All of the tests should run. We expect to see a few failures, since some of the tests from the previous chapters were intended to fail, for illustrative purposes. There's one failure, as shown in the following screenshot, though, that we need to consider:

```
======================================================================
FAIL: Doctest: PID.txt
----------------------------------------------------------------------
Traceback (most recent call last):
  File "/usr/lib64/python3.4/doctest.py", line 2193, in runTest
    raise self.failureException(self.format_failure(new.getvalue()))
AssertionError: Failed doctest test for PID.txt
  File "/ch6/project/test_chapter3/PID.txt", line 0

----------------------------------------------------------------------
File "/ch6/project/test_chapter3/PID.txt", line 16, in PID.txt
Failed example:
    controller.previous_time
Expected:
    1.0
Got:
    1403886575.9722168
```

The first part of this error report can be safely ignored: it just means that the whole `doctest` file is being treated as a failing test by Nose. The useful information comes in the second part of the report. It tells us that where we were expecting to get a previous time of `1.0`, instead we're getting a very large number (this will be different, and larger, when you run the test for yourself, as it represents the time in seconds since a point several decades in the past). What's going on? Didn't we replace `time.time` for that test with a mock? Let's take a look at the relevant part of `pid.txt`:

```
>>> import time
>>> real_time = time.time
>>> time.time = (float(x) for x in range(1, 1000)).__next__
>>> import pid
>>> controller = pid.PID(P = 0.5, I = 0.5, D = 0.5, setpoint = 0,
...                      initial = 12)
```

```
>>> controller.gains
(0.5, 0.5, 0.5)
>>> controller.setpoint
[0.0]
>>> controller.previous_time
1.0
```

We mocked `time.time`, sure enough (although it would be better to use the `unittest.mock patch` function). How is it that `from time import time` in `pid.py` is getting the wrong (which is to say, real) time function? What if `pid.py` had already been imported before this test ran? Then `from time import time` would already have been run before our mock was put in place, and it would never know about the mock. So, was `pid.py` imported by some thing else, before `pid.txt` imported it? As it happens, it was: Nose itself imported it, when it was scanning for tests to be executed. If we're using Nose, we can't count on our `import` statements actually being the first to import any given module. We can fix the problem easily, though, by using patch to replace the `time` function where our test code finds it:

```
>>> from unittest.mock import Mock, patch
>>> import pid
>>> with patch('pid.time', Mock(side_effect = [1.0, 2.0, 3.0])):
...     controller = pid.PID(P = 0.5, I = 0.5, D = 0.5, setpoint = 0,
...                          initial = 12)
>>> controller.gains
(0.5, 0.5, 0.5)
>>> controller.setpoint
[0.0]
>>> controller.previous_time
1.0
```

> Note that we're only looking at the first test in the file here. There is another test that would be better written in the same way, although it does pass. Can you spot that test and improve it?

Don't get confused: we switched to using `unittest.mock` for this test because it's a better tool for mocking objects, not because it solves the problem. The real solution is that we switched from replacing `time.time` to replacing `pid.time`. Nothing in `pid.py` refers to `time.time`, except for the `import` line. Every other place in the code that references `time` looks it up in the module's own global scope. That means it's `pid.time` that we really need to mock, and it always was. The fact that `pid.time` is another name for `time.time` is irrelevant; we should mock the object where it's found, not where it came from.

Now, when we run the tests again, the only failures are the expected ones. Your summary report (that we get because we passed -v to Nose on the command line) should look like this:

```
Doctest: inline_doctest.testable ... ok
Doctest: AVL.txt ... ok
Doctest: test.txt ... FAIL
Doctest: PID.txt ... ok
test_assertAlmostEqual (test_assertAlmostEqual.floating_point_problems) ... ok
test_assertEqual (test_assertAlmostEqual.floating_point_problems) ... FAIL
test_int_from_string (test_assertRaises.silly_int_test) ... FAIL
test_assertEqual (test_assertTrue.two_failing_tests) ... FAIL
test_assertTrue (test_assertTrue.two_failing_tests) ... FAIL
test_add_employee (test_employees.test_employees) ... ok
test_find_employee_by_date (test_employees.test_employees) ... ok
test_find_employees_by_name (test_employees.test_employees) ... ok
test_less_than (test_fail.test_with_fail) ... ok
test_with_when (test_pid.test_pid_calculate_response) ... ok
test_without_when (test_pid.test_pid_calculate_response) ... ok
test_with_when (test_pid.test_pid_constructor) ... ok
test_without_when (test_pid.test_pid_constructor) ... ok
```

We just saw how hidden assumptions can break tests, just as they can break the code being tested. Until now, we've been assuming that, when one of our tests imports a module, that's the first time the module has been imported. Some of our tests relied on this assumption to replace library objects with mocks. Now that we're dealing with running many tests aggregated together, with no guaranteed order of execution, this assumption isn't reliable. On top of that, the module that we had trouble with actually had to be imported to search it for tests, before any of our tests were run. A quick switch of the affected tests to use a better approach, and we were good to go.

So, we just ran all of these tests with a single command, and we can spread our tests across as many directories, source files, and documents as we need to keep everything organized. That's pretty nice. We're getting to the point where testing is useful in the real world.

We can store our tests in a separate and well-organized directory structure, and run them all with a single, quick, and simple command. We can also easily run a subset of our tests by passing the filenames, module names, or directories containing the tests we want to run as command-line parameters.

Simplifying the Nose command line

The `python3 -m nose` command that we used earlier was not hard to understand, but it's longer than we'd like if we're going to be typing it all the time. Instead of the following command:

```
python3 -m nose --with-doctest --doctest-extension=txt -v
```

We'd really prefer just the following command:

```
python3 -m nose
```

or, even more simply:

```
nosetests
```

Fortunately, it's simple to tell Nose that we want it to use different defaults for the values of these command-line switches. To do this, just create a configuration file called `nose.cfg` or `.noserc` (either name will work) in your home directory, and place the following inside it:

```
[nosetests]
with-doctest=1
doctest-extension=txtIf you're a Windows user, you might not be
sure what the phrase "home directory" is supposed to denote in
this context. As far as Python is concerned, your home directory is
defined by your environment variables. If HOME is defined, that's
your home directory. Otherwise, if USERPROFILE is defined (it usually
is, pointing at C:\Documents and Settings\USERNAME) then that is
considered to be your home directory. Otherwise, the directory
described by HOMEDRIVE and HOMEPATH (often C:\)is your home directory.
```

Setting the options in the configuration file takes care of all the extraneous command-line arguments. From now on, whenever you run Nose, it will assume these options, unless you tell it otherwise. You don't have to type them on the command line any more. You can use the same trick for any option that Nose can accept on the command line.

For the second refinement, Nose installs a script called `nosetests` when it's installed. Typing `nosetests` is exactly the same as typing `python3 -m nose`, except that you might have to add the directory that contains `nosetests` to your `PATH` environment variable before it will work. We'll continue using `python3 -m nose` in the examples.

Customizing Nose's test search

We've said before that Nose uses names of directories, modules, and functions to inform its search for tests. Directories and modules whose names start with `test` or `Test`, or contain a _, ., or - followed by `test` or `Test` will be included in the search, in addition to any other places that Nose decides it should search. This is by default, but it's not actually the whole story.

If you know about regular expressions, you can customize the pattern that Nose uses to look for tests. You can do this by passing the `--include=REGEX` command line option, or by putting `include=REGEX` in your `nose.cfg` or `.noserc`.

For example, run the following command:

```
python3 -m nose --include="(?:^[Dd]oc)"
```

Now Nose will, in addition to looking for names using the word `test`, also look for names that start with `doc` or `Doc`. This means that you can call the directory containing your `doctest` files as `docs`, `Documentation`, `doctests`, and so on, and Nose will still find and run those tests. If you use this option often, you'll almost certainly want to add it to your configuration file, as described under the previous heading.

> The full syntax and use of regular expressions is a subject itself, and has been the topic of many books; but you can find everything that you need to do in the Python documentation at `https://docs.python.org/3/library/re.html`.

Check your understanding

By running `python3 -m nose --processes=4`, Nose can be made to launch four testing processes simultaneously, which can be a big gain, if you're running the tests on a quad-core system. How would you make Nose always launch four testing processes, without being told on the command line? The answer is just put `processes=4` in your Nose configuration file.

If some of your tests were stored in a directory called `specs`, how would you tell Nose that it should search that directory for tests? You need to add `--include="specs"` to the Nose command line.

Which of the following will be recognized by Nose as possibly containing the `UnitTests`, `unit_tests`, `TestFiles`, `test_files`, and `doctests` tests by default? The answer is that `unit_tests`, `TestFiles`, and `test_files` will be recognized by Nose's default configuration.

Practicing Nose

Write some `doctest` and `unittest` tests for the following specification, and create a directory tree to contain them and the code that they describe. Write the code using the test-driven methodology, and use Nose to run the tests:

```
The graph module contains two classes: Node and Arc. An Arc is a
connection between two Nodes. Each Node is an intersection of an
arbitrary number of Arcs.

Arc objects contain references to the Node objects that the Arc
connects, a textual identification label, and a "cost" or "weight",
which is a real number.

Node objects contain references to all of the connected Arcs, and a
textual identification label.

Node objects have a find_cycle(self, length) method which returns a
list of Arcs making up the lowest cost complete path from the Node
back to itself, if such a path exists with a length greater than 2
Arcs and less than or equal to the length parameter.

Node and Arc objects have a __repr__(self) method which returns a
representation involving the identification labels assigned to the
objects.
```

Nose and doctest tests

Nose doesn't just support `doctest`, it actually enhances it. When you're using Nose, you can write test fixtures for your `doctest` files.

If you pass `--doctest-fixtures=_fixture` on the command line, Nose will go looking for a fixture file whenever it finds a `doctest` file. The name of the fixture file is based on the name of the `doctest` file, and is calculated by appending the `doctest` fixture suffix (in other words, the value of `doctest-fixtures`) to the main part of the `doctest` filename, and then adding `.py` to the end. For example, if Nose found a `doctest` file called `PID.txt`, and had been told to find `doctest-fixtures=_fixture`, it would try to find the test fixture in a file called `PID_fixture.py`.

The test fixture file for a `doctest` is very simple: it's just a Python module that contains a `setup()` or `setUp()` function, and a `teardown()` or `tearDown()` function. The `setup` function is executed before the `doctest` file, and the `teardown` function is executed after the `doctest` file.

The fixture operates in a different namespace from the `doctest` file, so none of the variables that get defined in the fixture module are visible in the actual tests. If you want to share the variables between the fixture and the test, you'll probably want to do it by making a simple little module to hold the variables, which you can import into both the fixture and the test.

Nose and unittest tests

Nose enhances `unittest` by providing test fixtures at the package and module levels. The package `setup` function is run before any of the tests in any of the modules in a package, while the `teardown` function is run after all of the tests in all of the modules in the package have completed. Similarly, the module `setup` function is run before any of the tests in a given module have been executed, and the module `teardown` function is executed after all of the tests in the module have been executed.

Module fixture practice

We're going to build a test module with a module-level fixture. In the fixture, we'll replace the `datetime.date.today` function, which normally returns an object representing the current date. We want it to return a specific value, so that our tests can know what to expect. Perform the following steps:

1. Create a directory called `tests`.
2. Within the `tests` directory, create a file called `module_fixture_tests.py` containing the following code:

```
from unittest import TestCase
from unittest.mock import patch, Mock
from datetime import date

fake_date = Mock()
fake_date.today = Mock(return_value = date(year = 2014,
                                           month = 6,
                                           day = 12))

patch_date = patch('module_fixture_tests.date', fake_date)


def setup():
    patch_date.start()

def teardown():
    patch_date.stop()
```

```
class first_tests(TestCase):
    def test_year(self):
        self.assertEqual(date.today().year, 2014)

    def test_month(self):
        self.assertEqual(date.today().month, 6)

    def test_day(self):
        self.assertEqual(date.today().day, 12)

class second_tests(TestCase):
    def test_isoformat(self):
        self.assertEqual(date.today().isoformat(), '2014-06-12')
```

3. Notice that there are two `TestCase` classes in this module. Using pure `unittest`, we'd have to duplicate the fixture code in each of these classes. Nose lets us write it once and use it in both the places.
4. Go ahead and run the tests by moving to the directory that contains the tests directory and type `python -m nose`.
5. Nose will recognize `tests` as a directory that might contain tests (because of the directory name), find the `module_fixtures_tests.py` file, run the `setup` function, run all of the tests, and then run the `teardown` function. There won't be much to see, though, aside from a simple report of how many tests passed.

You might have noticed yet another way of using `unittest.mock.patch` in the previous example. In addition to being usable as a decorator or a context manager, you can also use the `patch` function as a constructor, and call `start` and `stop` on the object it returns. Of all the ways you can use the `patch` function, this is the one to avoid in most cases, because this requires you to be careful to remember to call the `stop` function. The preceding code would have been better using `patch_date` as a class decorator on each of the `TestCase` classes, except that the point here was to demonstrate what module-level fixtures look like.

Normally, rather than creating mock objects, `setup` and `teardown` will do things such as handle, create, and destroy temporary files, or so on.

We can save ourselves some time and effort by using a second layer of test fixtures that wrap around the entire test modules instead of single test methods. By doing this, we save ourselves from duplicating the fixture code inside every test class in the module; but this comes with a cost. The `setup` and `teardown` functions aren't run before and after each test, as normal test fixtures are. Instead, all of the tests in the module happen between a single module-level setup/teardown pair, which means that, if a test does something that affects the environment created by the `setup` function, it won't be undone before the next test runs. In other words, the isolation of tests is not guaranteed with respect to the environment created by a module-level fixture.

Package fixture practice

Now, we're going to create a fixture that wraps around all the test modules in an entire package. Perform the following steps:

1. Add a new file called `__init__.py` to the `tests` directory that we created in the last practice section. (That's two underscores, the word `init` and two more underscores). The presence of this file tells Python that the directory is a package.
2. In `module_fixture_tests.py`, change:

   ```
   patch_date = patch('module_fixture_tests.date', fake_date)
   ```

   with the following:

   ```
   patch_date = patch('tests.module_fixture_tests.date', fake_date)
   ```

3. Place the following code inside `__init__.py` in the `tests` directory:

   ```
   from os import unlink

   def setup():
       with open('test.tmp', 'w') as f:
           f.write('This is a test file.')

   def teardown():
       unlink('test.tmp')
   ```

   > It's fairly common that the `__init__.py` files are completely empty, but they're the canonical source for the package object; so that's where Nose looks for a package-level fixture.

4. Add a new file called `package_fixtures_tests.py` to the `tests` directory, with the following contents:

   ```
   from unittest import TestCase
   from glob import glob

   class check_file_exists(TestCase):
       def test_glob(self):
           self.assertIn('test.tmp', glob('*.tmp'))
   ```

5. Go ahead and run the tests again. You won't see much output, but that just means the tests passed. Notice that the `test_glob` function can't succeed unless `test.tmp` exists. Since this file is created in the package setup and destroyed in the package teardown (and it no longer exists), we know that the setup was run before the test, and teardown was run after the test. If we added a test to `module_fixture_tests.py` that depended on `test.tmp`, they too would pass, because the `setup` function is called before any test in the package, and `teardown` is called after every test in the package has run.

> The `glob` module provides the ability to expand command-line - style wildcards into a list of filenames. The `glob.glob` function is one of several globbing functions available.

We worked with yet another layer of test fixture, this time wrapping around all of the test modules in the `tests` directory. As you can see from looking at the code we just wrote, the environment created by the package-level test fixture is available in every test in every module in the package.

Like module-level test fixtures, package-level test fixtures can be a big labor-saving shortcut, but they don't provide you with the protection against communication between tests that real test-level fixtures do.

> Why did we change `'module_fixture_tests.date'` into `'tests.module_fixture_tests.date'` when we added the package-level fixture? Well, when we added `__init__.py` to the `tests` directory, in Python's view, we changed that directory into a Python package. As a Python package, its name is part of the absolute name of any variable inside it, which indirectly includes our imported `date` class. We have to pass an absolute variable name to patch, so we have to start with the containing package name.

Nose and ad hoc tests

Nose supports two new kinds of tests: standalone test functions, and non-`TestCase` test classes. It finds these tests by using the same pattern matching that it uses to find test modules. When looking through a module whose name matches the pattern, any functions or classes whose names also match the pattern are assumed to be tests.

We're going to write a few tests that demonstrate Nose's support for test functions and non-`TestCase` test classes.

Let's create a new test file in the `tests` directory, called `nose_specific_tests.py`. Inside the file, put the following code:

```
import sys
from sqlite3 import connect
from imp import reload

class grouped_tests:
    def setup(self):
        self.connection = connect(':memory:')
        cursor = self.connection.cursor()
        cursor.execute('create table test (a, b, c)')
        cursor.execute('''insert into test (a, b, c)
                          values (1, 2, 3)''')
        self.connection.commit()

    def teardown(self):
        self.connection.close()

    def test_update(self):
        cursor = self.connection.cursor()
        cursor.execute('update test set b = 7 where a = 1')

    def test_select(self):
        cursor = self.connection.cursor()
        cursor.execute('select * from test limit 1')
        assert cursor.fetchone() == (1, 2, 3)

def platform_setup():
    sys.platform = 'test platform'

def platform_teardown():
    global sys
    sys = reload(sys)

def standalone_test():
    assert sys.platform == 'test platform'

standalone_test.setup = platform_setup
standalone_test.teardown = platform_teardown
```

Running Nose now doesn't print out very much, but the fact that the tests were run and didn't fail tells us a lot.

The `grouped_tests` class contains a test fixture (the `setup` and `teardown` methods) and two tests; but it's not a `unittest TestCase` class. Nose recognized it as a test class because its name follows the same pattern that Nose looks for when it checks module names to find test modules. It then looks through the class for a test fixture and any test methods, and runs them appropriately.

Since the class isn't a `TestCase` class, the tests don't have access to any of the `unittest assert` methods; Nose considers such a test to pass unless it raises an exception. Python has an `assert` statement that raises an exception if its expression is false, which is helpful for just this sort of thing. It's not as nice as `assertEqual`, but it does the job in many cases.

We wrote another test in the `standalone_test` function. Like `grouped_tests`, `standalone_test` is recognized as a test by Nose because its name matches the same pattern that Nose uses to search for test modules. Nose runs `standalone_test` as a test, and reports a failure if it raises an exception.

We were able to attach a test fixture to `standalone_test` by setting its `setup` and `teardown` attributes to a pair of functions that we defined for that purpose. As usual, the `setup` function runs before the test function and the `teardown` function runs after the test function.

Summary

We learned a lot in this chapter about the Nose testing meta-framework. Specifically, we covered how Nose finds files that contain tests, and how you can adapt the process to fit into your organization scheme; how to run all of your tests with Nose, whether they are `doctest`, `unittest`, or ad hoc; how Nose enhances the other frameworks with additional support for test fixtures; and how to use Nose's support for standalone test functions and non-`TestCase` test classes.

Now that we've learned about Nose and running all of our tests easily, we're ready to tackle a complete test-driven project, which is the topic of the next chapter.

7

Test-driven Development Walk-through

In this chapter, we're not going to talk about new techniques of testing in Python, and we're not going to spend much time talking about the philosophy of testing. Instead, what we're going to do is a step-by-step walk-through of an actual development process. Your humble and sadly fallible author has commemorated his mistakes—and the ways that testing helped him fix them—while developing part of a personal scheduling program.

In this chapter, we'll cover the following topics:

- Writing a testable specification
- Writing unit tests that drive the development process
- Writing code that complies with the specification and unit tests
- Using the testable specification and unit tests to help debug

You'll be prompted to design and build your own module as you read through this chapter, so that you can walk through your own process as well.

Writing the specification

As usual, the process starts with a written specification. The specification is a `doctest` that we learned in *Chapter 2, Working with doctest*, and *Chapter 3, Unit Testing with doctest*, so the computer can use it to check the implementation. The specification isn't strictly a set of unit tests, though the discipline of unit testing has been sacrificed (for the moment) in exchange for making the document more accessible to a human reader. That's a common trade-off, and it's fine as long as you make up for it by also writing unit tests covering the code.

The goal of the project in this chapter is to make a Python package capable of representing personal time management information.

The following code goes in a file called `docs/outline.txt`:

```
This project is a personal scheduling system intended to keep track of
a single person's schedule and activities. The system will store and
display two kinds of schedule information: activities and statuses.
Activities and statuses both support a protocol which allows them to
be checked for overlap with another object supporting the protocol.

>>> from planner.data import Activity, Status
>>> from datetime import datetime

Activities and statuses are stored in schedules, to which they can be
added and removed.

>>> from planner.data import Schedule
>>> activity = Activity('test activity',
..                      datetime(year = 2014, month = 6, day = 1,
..                               hour = 10, minute = 15),
..                      datetime(year = 2014, month = 6, day = 1,
..                               hour = 12, minute = 30))
>>> duplicate_activity = Activity('test activity',
..                      datetime(year = 2014, month = 6, day = 1,
..                               hour = 10, minute = 15),
..                      datetime(year = 2014, month = 6, day = 1,
..                               hour = 12, minute = 30))
>>> status = Status('test status',
...                 datetime(year = 2014, month = 7, day = 1,
...                          hour = 10, minute = 15),
...                 datetime(year = 2014, month = 7, day = 1,
...                          hour = 12, minute = 30))
>>> schedule = Schedule()
>>> schedule.add(activity)
>>> schedule.add(status)
>>> status in schedule
True
>>> activity in schedule
True
>>> duplicate_activity in schedule
True
>>> schedule.remove(activity)
>>> schedule.remove(status)
>>> status in schedule
```

```
False
>>> activity in schedule
False

Activities represent tasks that the person must actively engage in,
and they are therefore mutually exclusive: no person can have two
activities that overlap the same period of time.

>>> activity1 = Activity('test activity 1',
...                          datetime(year = 2014, month = 6, day = 1,
...                                   hour = 9, minute = 5),
...                          datetime(year = 2014, month = 6, day = 1,
...                                   hour = 12, minute = 30))
>>> activity2 = Activity('test activity 2',
...                          datetime(year = 2014, month = 6, day = 1,
...                                   hour = 10, minute = 15),
...                          datetime(year = 2014, month = 6, day = 1,
...                                   hour = 13, minute = 30))
>>> schedule = Schedule()
>>> schedule.add(activity1)
>>> schedule.add(activity2)
Traceback (most recent call last):
ScheduleError: "test activity 2" overlaps with "test activity 1"

Statuses represent tasks that a person engages in passively, and so
can overlap with each other and with activities.

>>> activity1 = Activity('test activity 1',
...                          datetime(year = 2014, month = 6, day = 1,
...                                   hour = 9, minute = 5),
...                          datetime(year = 2014, month = 6, day = 1,
...                                   hour = 12, minute = 30))
>>> status1 = Status('test status 1',
...                      datetime(year = 2014, month = 6, day = 1,
...                               hour = 10, minute = 15),
...                      datetime(year = 2014, month = 6, day = 1,
...                               hour = 13, minute = 30))
>>> status2 = Status('test status 2',
...                      datetime(year = 2014, month = 6, day = 1,
...                               hour = 8, minute = 45),
...                      datetime(year = 2014, month = 6, day = 1,
...                               hour = 15, minute = 30))
>>> schedule = Schedule()
>>> schedule.add(activity1)
```

```
>>> schedule.add(status1)
>>> schedule.add(status2)
>>> activity1 in schedule
True
>>> status1 in schedule
True
>>> status2 in schedule
True

Schedules can be saved to a sqlite database, and they can be reloaded
from that stored state.

>>> from planner.persistence import file
>>> storage = File(':memory:')
>>> schedule.store(storage)
>>> newsched = Schedule.load(storage)
>>> schedule == newsched
True
```

This `doctest` will serve as a testable specification for my project, which means that it will be the foundation stone for all of my tests and my program code that will be built on. Let's look at each section in more detail:

```
This project is a personal scheduling system intended to keep track of
a single person's schedule and activities. The system will store and
display two kinds of schedule information: activities and statuses.
Activities and statuses both support a protocol which allows them to
be checked for overlap with another object supporting the protocol.

>>> from planner.data import Activity, Status
>>> from datetime import datetime
```

The preceding code consists of some introductory English text, and a couple of `import` statements that bring in code that we need for these tests. By doing so, they also tell us about some of the structure of the `planner` package. It contains a module called `data` that defines `Activity` and `Status`.

```
Activities and statuses are stored in schedules, to which they can be
added and removed.

>>> from planner.data import Schedule
>>> activity = Activity('test activity',
..                      datetime(year = 2014, month = 6, day = 1,
..                               hour = 10, minute = 15),
..                      datetime(year = 2014, month = 6, day = 1,
```

```
..                                      hour = 12, minute = 30))
>>> duplicate_activity = Activity('test activity',
..                            datetime(year = 2014, month = 6, day = 1,
..                                     hour = 10, minute = 15),
..                            datetime(year = 2014, month = 6, day = 1,
..                                     hour = 12, minute = 30))
>>> status = Status('test status',
...                       datetime(year = 2014, month = 7, day = 1,
...                                hour = 10, minute = 15),
...                       datetime(year = 2014, month = 7, day = 1,
...                                hour = 12, minute = 30))
>>> schedule = Schedule()
>>> schedule.add(activity)
>>> schedule.add(status)
>>> status in schedule
True
>>> activity in schedule
True
>>> duplicate_activity in schedule
True
>>> schedule.remove(activity)
>>> schedule.remove(status)
>>> status in schedule
False
>>> activity in schedule
False
```

The preceding tests describe some of the desired behavior of `the Schedule` instances when interacting with the `Activity` and `Status` objects. According to these tests, a `Schedule` instance must accept an `Activity` or `Status` object as the parameter of its `add` and `remove` methods; once added, the `in` operator must return `True` for an object until it is removed. Furthermore, the two `Activity` instances that have the same parameters must be treated as the same object by `Schedule`:

```
Activities represent tasks that the person must actively engage in,
and they are therefore mutually exclusive: no person can have two
activities that overlap the same period of time.

>>> activity1 = Activity('test activity 1',
...                         datetime(year = 2014, month = 6, day = 1,
...                                  hour = 9, minute = 5),
...                         datetime(year = 2014, month = 6, day = 1,
...                                  hour = 12, minute = 30))
>>> activity2 = Activity('test activity 2',
...                         datetime(year = 2014, month = 6, day = 1,
```

```
...                                    hour = 10, minute = 15),
...                           datetime(year = 2014, month = 6, day = 1,
...                                    hour = 13, minute = 30))
>>> schedule = Schedule()
>>> schedule.add(activity1)
>>> schedule.add(activity2)
Traceback (most recent call last):
ScheduleError: "test activity 2" overlaps with "test activity 1"
```

The preceding test code describes what should happen when overlapping activities are added to a schedule. Specifically, a `ScheduleError` exception should be raised:

```
Statuses represent tasks that a person engages in passively, and so
can overlap with each other and with activities.

>>> activity1 = Activity('test activity 1',
...                           datetime(year = 2014, month = 6, day = 1,
...                                    hour = 9, minute = 5),
...                           datetime(year = 2014, month = 6, day = 1,
...                                    hour = 12, minute = 30))
>>> status1 = Status('test status 1',
...                       datetime(year = 2014, month = 6, day = 1,
...                                hour = 10, minute = 15),
...                       datetime(year = 2014, month = 6, day = 1,
...                                hour = 13, minute = 30))
>>> status2 = Status('test status 2',
...                       datetime(year = 2014, month = 6, day = 1,
...                                hour = 8, minute = 45),
...                       datetime(year = 2014, month = 6, day = 1,
...                                hour = 15, minute = 30))
>>> schedule = Schedule()
>>> schedule.add(activity1)
>>> schedule.add(status1)
>>> schedule.add(status2)
>>> activity1 in schedule
True
>>> status1 in schedule
True
>>> status2 in schedule
True
```

The preceding test code describes what should happen when overlapping statuses are added to a schedule: the schedule should accept them. Furthermore, if a status and an activity overlap, they can still both be added:

```
Schedules can be saved to a sqlite database, and they can be reloaded
from that stored state.

>>> from planner.persistence import file
>>> storage = File(':memory:')
>>> schedule.store(storage)
>>> newsched = Schedule.load(storage)
>>> schedule == newsched
True
```

The preceding code describes how schedule storage should work. It also tells us that the `planner` package needs to contain a `persistence` module that, in turn, should contain `File`. It also tells us that `Schedule` instances should have `load` and `store` methods, and that the `==` operator should return `True` when they contain the same data.

Try it for yourself – what are you going to do?

It's time for you to come up with a project of your own, something you can work on for yourself. We step through the development process:

1. Think of a project of approximately the same complexity as the one described in this chapter. It should be a single module or a few modules in a single package. It should also be something that interests you, which is why I haven't given you a specific assignment here.

   Imagine that the project is already done, and you need to write a description of what you've done, along with a little bit of demonstration code. Then go ahead and write your description and demo code in the form of a `doctest` file.

2. As you're writing the `doctest` file, watch out for places where your original idea has to change a little bit to make the demo easier to write or work better. When you find such cases, pay attention to them! At this stage, it's better to change the idea a little bit and save yourself effort all through the process.

Wrapping up the specification

We've now got testable specifications for a couple of moderately-sized projects—yours and mine. These will help us to write unit tests and code, and they'll give us a sense of how complete each project is as a whole.

In addition, the process of writing code into the `doctest` gave us a chance to test-drive our ideas. We've probably improved on our projects a little bit by using them in a concrete manner, even though the project implementation is still merely imaginary.

Once again, it's important that we have these tests written before writing the code that they will test. By writing the tests first, we give ourselves a touchstone that we can use in order to judge how well our code conforms to what we intended. If we write the code first, and then the tests, all we end up doing is enshrining what the code actually does—as opposed to what we meant for it to do—into the tests.

Writing initial unit tests

Since the specification doesn't contain unit tests, there's still a need for unit tests before the coding of the module can begin. The `planner.data` classes are the first target for the implementation, so they're the first ones to get the tests.

Activities and statuses are defined to be very similar, so their test modules are also similar. They're not identical, though, and they're not required to have any particular inheritance relationship; so the tests remain distinct.

The following tests are in `tests/test_activities.py`:

```
from unittest import TestCase
from unittest.mock import patch, Mock
from planner.data import Activity, TaskError
from datetime import datetime

class constructor_tests(TestCase):
    def test_valid(self):
        activity = Activity('activity name',
                            datetime(year = 2012, month = 9, day = 11),
                            datetime(year = 2013, month = 4, day = 27))

        self.assertEqual(activity.name, 'activity name')
        self.assertEqual(activity.begins,
                         datetime(year = 2012, month = 9, day = 11))
        self.assertEqual(activity.ends,
                         datetime(year = 2013, month = 4, day = 27))

    def test_backwards_times(self):
        self.assertRaises(TaskError,
                          Activity,
                          'activity name',
```

```
                              datetime(year = 2013, month = 4, day = 27),
                              datetime(year = 2012, month = 9, day = 11))

    def test_too_short(self):
        self.assertRaises(TaskError,
                              Activity,
                              'activity name',
                              datetime(year = 2013, month = 4, day = 27,
                                       hour = 7, minute = 15),
                              datetime(year = 2013, month = 4, day = 27,
                                       hour = 7, minute = 15))

class utility_tests(TestCase):
    def test_repr(self):
        activity = Activity('activity name',
                               datetime(year = 2012, month = 9, day = 11),
                               datetime(year = 2013, month = 4, day = 27))

        expected = "<activity name 2012-09-11T00:00:00 2013-04-
27T00:00:00>"

        self.assertEqual(repr(activity), expected)

class exclusivity_tests(TestCase):
    def test_excludes(self):
        activity = Mock()

        other = Activity('activity name',
                            datetime(year = 2012, month = 9, day = 11),
                            datetime(year = 2012, month = 10, day = 6))

        # Any activity should exclude any activity
        self.assertTrue(Activity.excludes(activity, other))

        # Anything not known to be excluded should be included
        self.assertFalse(Activity.excludes(activity, None))

class overlap_tests(TestCase):
    def test_overlap_before(self):
        activity = Mock(begins = datetime(year = 2012, month = 9,
        day = 11),
                        ends = datetime(year = 2012, month = 10,
                        day = 6))
```

```
        other = Mock(begins = datetime(year = 2012, month = 10,
        day = 7),
                     ends = datetime(year = 2013, month = 2, day = 5))

        self.assertFalse(Activity.overlaps(activity, other))

    def test_overlap_begin(self):
        activity = Mock(begins = datetime(year = 2012, month = 8,
        day = 11),
                        ends = datetime(year = 2012, month = 11,
                        day = 27))

        other = Mock(begins = datetime(year = 2012, month = 10,
        day = 7),
                     ends = datetime(year = 2013, month = 2, day = 5))

        self.assertTrue(Activity.overlaps(activity, other))

    def test_overlap_end(self):
        activity = Mock(begins = datetime(year = 2013, month = 1,
        day = 11),
                        ends = datetime(year = 2013, month = 4,
                        day = 16))

        other = Mock(begins = datetime(year = 2012, month = 10,
        day = 7),
                     ends = datetime(year = 2013, month = 2, day = 5))

        self.assertTrue(Activity.overlaps(activity, other))

    def test_overlap_inner(self):
        activity = Mock(begins = datetime(year = 2012, month = 10,
        day = 11),
                        ends = datetime(year = 2013, month = 1,
                        day = 27))

        other = Mock(begins = datetime(year = 2012, month = 10,
        day = 7),
                     ends = datetime(year = 2013, month = 2, day = 5))
```

```
        self.assertTrue(Activity.overlaps(activity, other))

    def test_overlap_outer(self):
        activity = Mock(begins = datetime(year = 2012, month = 8,
        day = 12),
                        ends = datetime(year = 2013, month = 3,
                        day = 15))

        other = Mock(begins = datetime(year = 2012, month = 10,
        day = 7),
                     ends = datetime(year = 2013, month = 2, day = 5))

        self.assertTrue(Activity.overlaps(activity, other))

    def test_overlap_after(self):
        activity = Mock(begins = datetime(year = 2013, month = 2,
        day = 6),
                        ends = datetime(year = 2013, month = 4,
                        day = 27))

        other = Mock(begins = datetime(year = 2012, month = 10,
        day = 7),
                     ends = datetime(year = 2013, month = 2, day = 5))

        self.assertFalse(Activity.overlaps(activity, other))
```

Let's take a look at the following code, step-by-step:

```
    def test_valid(self):
        activity = Activity('activity name',
                            datetime(year = 2012, month = 9,
                            day = 11),
                            datetime(year = 2013, month = 4,
                            day = 27))

        self.assertEqual(activity.name, 'activity name')
        self.assertEqual(activity.begins,
                         datetime(year = 2012, month = 9, day = 11))
        self.assertEqual(activity.ends,
                         datetime(year = 2013, month = 4, day = 27))
```

The `test_valid` method checks whether the constructor works correctly when all of the parameters are correct. This is an important test, because it defines what correct behavior should be normally. We need more tests, though, to define correct behavior in abnormal situations:

```
    def test_backwards_times(self):
        self.assertRaises(TaskError,
                          Activity,
                          'activity name',
                          datetime(year = 2013, month = 4, day = 27),
                          datetime(year = 2012, month = 9, day = 11))
```

Here, we're making sure that you can't create an activity that ends before it begins. That doesn't make any sense, and can easily throw off assumptions made during the implementation:

```
    def test_too_short(self):
        self.assertRaises(TaskError,
                          Activity,
                          'activity name',
                          datetime(year = 2013, month = 4, day = 27,
                                   hour = 7, minute = 15),
                          datetime(year = 2013, month = 4, day = 27,
                                   hour = 7, minute = 15))
```

We don't want extremely short activities, either. In the real world, an activity that takes no time is meaningless, so we have a test here to make sure that such things are not allowed:

```
class utility_tests(TestCase):
    def test_repr(self):
        activity = Activity('activity name',
                            datetime(year = 2012, month = 9,
                            day = 11),
                            datetime(year = 2013, month = 4,
                            day = 27))

        expected = "<activity name 2012-09-11T00:00:00 2013-04-
27T00:00:00>"

        self.assertEqual(repr(activity), expected)
```

While `repr(activity)` isn't likely to be used in any production code paths, it's handy during development and debugging. This test defines how the text representation of an activity ought to look, to make sure that it contains the desired information.

> The `repr` function is often useful during debugging, because it attempts to take any object and turn it into a string that represents that object. This is distinct from the `str` function, because `str` tries to turn the object into a string that is convenient for humans to read. The `repr` function, on the other hand, tries to create a string containing code that will recreate the object. That's a slightly tough concept, so here's an example contrasting `str` and `repr`:
>
> ```
> >>> from decimal import Decimal
> >>> x = Decimal('123.45678')
> >>> str(x)
> '123.45678'
> >>> repr(x)
> "Decimal('123.45678')"
> ```

```
class exclusivity_tests(TestCase):
    def test_excludes(self):
        activity = Mock()

        other = Activity('activity name',
                         datetime(year = 2012, month = 9, day = 11),
                         datetime(year = 2012, month = 10, day = 6))

        # Any activity should exclude any activity
        self.assertTrue(Activity.excludes(activity, other))

        # Anything not known to be excluded should be included
        self.assertFalse(Activity.excludes(activity, None))
```

It's up to the objects stored in a schedule to decide whether they are exclusive with other objects they overlap. Specifically, activities are supposed to exclude each other, so we check this here. We're using a mock object for the main activity, but we're being a bit lazy and use a real `Activity` instance to compare it against, trusting that there won't be a problem in this case. We don't expect that `Activity.excludes` will do much more than apply the `isinstance` function to its parameter, so there's not much that an error in the constructor can do to mess things up.

```
class overlap_tests(TestCase):
    def test_overlap_before(self):
```

```
        activity = Mock(begins = datetime(year = 2012, month = 9,
        day = 11),
                        ends = datetime(year = 2012, month = 10,
                        day = 6))

        other = Mock(begins = datetime(year = 2012, month = 10,
        day = 7),
                     ends = datetime(year = 2013, month = 2, day = 5))

        self.assertFalse(Activity.overlaps(activity, other))

    def test_overlap_begin(self):
        activity = Mock(begins = datetime(year = 2012, month = 8,
        day = 11),
                        ends = datetime(year = 2012, month = 11,
                        day = 27))

        other = Mock(begins = datetime(year = 2012, month = 10,
        day = 7),
                     ends = datetime(year = 2013, month = 2, day = 5))

        self.assertTrue(Activity.overlaps(activity, other))

    def test_overlap_end(self):
        activity = Mock(begins = datetime(year = 2013, month = 1,
        day = 11),
                        ends = datetime(year = 2013, month = 4,
                        day = 16))

        other = Mock(begins = datetime(year = 2012, month = 10,
        day = 7),
                     ends = datetime(year = 2013, month = 2, day = 5))

        self.assertTrue(Activity.overlaps(activity, other))

    def test_overlap_inner(self):
        activity = Mock(begins = datetime(year = 2012, month = 10,
        day = 11),
                        ends = datetime(year = 2013, month = 1,
                        day = 27))

        other = Mock(begins = datetime(year = 2012, month = 10,
        day = 7),
                     ends = datetime(year = 2013, month = 2, day = 5))

        self.assertTrue(Activity.overlaps(activity, other))
```

```
    def test_overlap_outer(self):
        activity = Mock(begins = datetime(year = 2012, month = 8,
        day = 12),
                        ends = datetime(year = 2013, month = 3,
                        day = 15))

        other = Mock(begins = datetime(year = 2012, month = 10,
        day = 7),
                     ends = datetime(year = 2013, month = 2, day = 5))

        self.assertTrue(Activity.overlaps(activity, other))

    def test_overlap_after(self):
        activity = Mock(begins = datetime(year = 2013, month = 2,
        day = 6),
                        ends = datetime(year = 2013, month = 4,
                        day = 27))

        other = Mock(begins = datetime(year = 2012, month = 10,
        day = 7),
                     ends = datetime(year = 2013, month = 2, day = 5))

        self.assertFalse(Activity.overlaps(activity, other))
```

These tests describe the behavior of the code that checks whether activities overlap in the cases where the first activity:

- Comes before the second activity
- Overlaps the beginning of the second activity
- Overlaps the end of the second activity
- Begins and ends within the range of the second activity
- Begins before the second activity and ends after it
- Comes after the second activity

This covers the domain of possible relationships between the tasks.

No actual activities were used in these tests, just `Mock` objects that had been given the attributes that the `Activity.overlaps` function should look for. As always, we're doing our best to keep the code in different units from being able to interact during the tests.

> You might have noticed that we used a shortcut to create the mock objects, by passing the attributes, we wanted them to have as keyword parameters for the constructor. Most of the time, that's a handy way to save a little work, but it does have the problem that it only works for attribute names that don't happen to be used as actual parameters to the `Mock` constructor. Notably, attributes called `name` can't be assigned in this way, because that parameter has a special meaning for `Mock`.

The code in `tests/test_statuses.py` is almost the same, except that it uses the `Status` class instead of the `Activity` class. There is one significant difference, though:

```
    def test_excludes(self):
        status = Mock()

        other = Status('status name',
                       datetime(year = 2012, month = 9, day = 11),
                       datetime(year = 2012, month = 10, day = 6))

        # A status shouldn't exclude anything
        self.assertFalse(Status.excludes(status, other))
        self.assertFalse(Status.excludes(status, None))
```

The defining difference between a `Status` and an `Activity` is that a status does not exclude other tasks that overlap with it. The tests, naturally, should reflect that difference.

The following code goes in `tests/test_schedules.py`. We define several mock objects that behave as if they were statuses or activities, and in which they support the overlap and exclusion protocol. We'll use these mock objects in several tests, to see how the schedule deals with the various combinations of overlapping and exclusive objects:

```
from unittest import TestCase
from unittest.mock import patch, Mock
from planner.data import Schedule, ScheduleError
from datetime import datetime

class add_tests(TestCase):
    overlap_exclude = Mock()
```

```
    overlap_exclude.overlaps = Mock(return_value = True)
    overlap_exclude.excludes = Mock(return_value = True)

    overlap_include = Mock()
    overlap_include.overlaps = Mock(return_value = True)
    overlap_include.excludes = Mock(return_value = False)

    distinct_exclude = Mock()
    distinct_exclude.overlaps = Mock(return_value = False)
    distinct_exclude.excludes = Mock(return_value = True)

    distinct_include = Mock()
    distinct_include.overlaps = Mock(return_value = False)
    distinct_include.excludes = Mock(return_value = False)

    def test_add_overlap_exclude(self):
        schedule = Schedule()
        schedule.add(self.distinct_include)
        self.assertRaises(ScheduleError,
                          schedule.add,
                          self.overlap_exclude)

    def test_add_overlap_include(self):
        schedule = Schedule()
        schedule.add(self.distinct_include)
        schedule.add(self.overlap_include)

    def test_add_distinct_exclude(self):
        schedule = Schedule()
        schedule.add(self.distinct_include)
        schedule.add(self.distinct_exclude)

    def test_add_distinct_include(self):
        schedule = Schedule()
        schedule.add(self.distinct_include)
        schedule.add(self.distinct_include)

    def test_add_over_overlap_exclude(self):
        schedule = Schedule()
        schedule.add(self.overlap_exclude)
        self.assertRaises(ScheduleError,
                          schedule.add,
                          self.overlap_include)

    def test_add_over_distinct_exclude(self):
        schedule = Schedule()
        schedule.add(self.distinct_exclude)
```

```
            self.assertRaises(ScheduleError,
                              schedule.add,
                              self.overlap_include)

        def test_add_over_overlap_include(self):
            schedule = Schedule()
            schedule.add(self.overlap_include)
            schedule.add(self.overlap_include)

        def test_add_over_distinct_include(self):
            schedule = Schedule()
            schedule.add(self.distinct_include)
            schedule.add(self.overlap_include)

    class in_tests(TestCase):
        fake = Mock()
        fake.overlaps = Mock(return_value = True)
        fake.excludes = Mock(return_value = True)

        def test_in_before_add(self):
            schedule = Schedule()
            self.assertFalse(self.fake in schedule)

        def test_in_after_add(self):
            schedule = Schedule()
            schedule.add(self.fake)
            self.assertTrue(self.fake in schedule)
```

Let's take a closer look at some sections of the following code:

```
        overlap_exclude = Mock()
        overlap_exclude.overlaps = Mock(return_value = True)
        overlap_exclude.excludes = Mock(return_value = True)

        overlap_include = Mock()
        overlap_include.overlaps = Mock(return_value = True)
        overlap_include.excludes = Mock(return_value = False)

        distinct_exclude = Mock()
        distinct_exclude.overlaps = Mock(return_value = False)
        distinct_exclude.excludes = Mock(return_value = True)

        distinct_include = Mock()
        distinct_include.overlaps = Mock(return_value = False)
        distinct_include.excludes = Mock(return_value = False)
```

These lines create mock objects as attributes of the `add_tests` class. Each of these mock objects has mocked `overlaps` and `excludes` methods that will always return either `True` or `False` when called. This means that each of these mock objects considers itself as overlap ping either everything or nothing, and excludes either everything or nothing. Between the four mock objects, we have covered all the possible combinations. In the following tests, we'll add various combinations of these mock objects to a schedule, and make sure that it does the right things:

```
    def test_add_overlap_exclude(self):
        schedule = Schedule()
        schedule.add(self.distinct_include)
        self.assertRaises(ScheduleError,
                          schedule.add,
                          self.overlap_exclude)

    def test_add_overlap_include(self):
        schedule = Schedule()
        schedule.add(self.distinct_include)
        schedule.add(self.overlap_include)

    def test_add_distinct_exclude(self):
        schedule = Schedule()
        schedule.add(self.distinct_include)
        schedule.add(self.distinct_exclude)

    def test_add_distinct_include(self):
        schedule = Schedule()
        schedule.add(self.distinct_include)
        schedule.add(self.distinct_include)
```

The preceding four tests are covering cases where we add a nonoverlapping object to a schedule. All of them are expected to accept the nonoverlapping object, except the first. In this test, we've previously added an object that claims that it does indeed overlap; furthermore, it excludes anything it overlaps. This test shows that, if either the object being added or an object already in the schedule believes that there's an overlap, the schedule must treat it as an overlap.

```
    def test_add_over_overlap_exclude(self):
        schedule = Schedule()
        schedule.add(self.overlap_exclude)
        self.assertRaises(ScheduleError,
                          schedule.add,
                          self.overlap_include)
```

In this test, we're making sure that if an object already in the schedule overlaps a new object and claims exclusivity, then adding the new object will fail.

```
    def test_add_over_distinct_exclude(self):
        schedule = Schedule()
        schedule.add(self.distinct_exclude)
        self.assertRaises(ScheduleError,
                          schedule.add,
                          self.overlap_include)
```

In this test, we're making sure that, even though the object already in the schedule doesn't think that it overlaps with the new object, it excludes the new object because the new object thinks that there's an overlap.

```
    def test_add_over_overlap_include(self):
        schedule = Schedule()
        schedule.add(self.overlap_include)
        schedule.add(self.overlap_include)

    def test_add_over_distinct_include(self):
        schedule = Schedule()
        schedule.add(self.distinct_include)
        schedule.add(self.overlap_include)
```

These tests are making sure that the inclusive objects don't somehow interfere with adding each other to a schedule.

```
class in_tests(TestCase):
    fake = Mock()
    fake.overlaps = Mock(return_value = True)
    fake.excludes = Mock(return_value = True)

    def test_in_before_add(self):
        schedule = Schedule()
        self.assertFalse(self.fake in schedule)

    def test_in_after_add(self):
        schedule = Schedule()
        schedule.add(self.fake)
        self.assertTrue(self.fake in schedule)
```

These two tests describe the schedule behavior with respect to the `in` operator. Specifically, it should return `True` when the object in question is actually in the schedule.

Try it for yourself – write your early unit tests

A specification—even a testable specification written in `doctest`—still hosts a lot of ambiguities that can be ironed out with good unit tests. Add that to the fact that the specification doesn't maintain separation between different tests, and you can see that it's time for your project to gain some unit tests. Perform the following steps:

1. Find some element of your project that is described in (or implied by) your specification.
2. Write a unit test that describes the behavior of that element when given the correct input.
3. Write a unit test that describes the behavior of that element when given the incorrect input.
4. Write unit tests that describe the behavior of the element at the boundaries between correct and incorrect input.
5. Go back to step 1 if you can find another untested part of your program.

Wrapping up the initial unit tests

This is where you really take what was an ill-defined idea and turn it into a precise description of what you're going to do.

The end result can be quite lengthy, which shouldn't come as much of a surprise. After all, your goal at this stage is to completely define the behavior of your project; even without concerning yourself with the details of how that behavior is implemented, that's a lot of information.

Coding planner.data

It's time to write some code using the specification document and the unit tests as guides. Specifically, it's time to write the `planner.data` module, which contains `Status`, `Activity`, and `Schedule`.

To create this package, I made a directory called `planner` and, within this directory, created a file called `__init__.py`. There's no need to put anything inside `__init__.py`, but the file itself needs to exist to tell Python that the `planner` directory is a package.

The following code goes in `planner/data.py`:

```
from datetime import timedelta

class TaskError(Exception):
```

```
    pass

class ScheduleError(Exception):
    pass

class Task:
    def __init__(self, name, begins, ends):
        if ends < begins:
            raise TaskError('The begin time must precede the end
time')
        if ends - begins < timedelta(minutes = 5):
            raise TaskError('The minimum duration is 5 minutes')

        self.name = name
        self.begins = begins
        self.ends = ends

    def excludes(self, other):
        return NotImplemented

    def overlaps(self, other):
        if other.begins < self.begins:
            return other.ends > self.begins
        elif other.ends > self.ends:
            return other.begins < self.ends
        else:
            return True

    def __repr__(self):
        return '<{} {} {}>'.format(self.name,
                                   self.begins.isoformat(),
                                   self.ends.isoformat())

class Activity(Task):
    def excludes(self, other):
        return isinstance(other, Activity)

class Status(Task):
    def excludes(self, other):
        return False

class Schedule:
    def __init__(self):
        self.tasks = []

    def add(self, task):
        for contained in self.tasks:
```

```
            if task.overlaps(contained):
                if task.exclude(contained) or contained.exclude(task):
                    raise ScheduleError(task, containeed)

        self.tasks.append(task)

    def remove(self, task):
        try:
            self.tasks.remove(task)
        except ValueError:
            pass

    def __contains__(self, task):
        return task in self.tasks
```

The `Task` class here contains most of the behavior that is needed for both the `Activity` class and the `Status` class. Since so much of what they do is common to both, it makes sense to write the code once and reuse it. Only the `excludes` method needs to be different in each of the subclasses. That makes the classes for activities and statuses very simple. The `Schedule` class turns out to be pretty easy, too. But is it right? Our tests will tell us.

> We used the `timedelta` class and the `datetime.isoformat` method in the preceding code. Both are useful but somewhat obscure features of the `datetime` module. A `timedelta` instance represents the duration between two points in time. The `isoformat` method returns a string representing the `datetime` module in ISO 8601 standard format.

Using tests to get the code right

All right, so that code looks fairly good. Unfortunately, Nose tells us that there are a few problems. Actually, Nose reports quite a large number of problems, but a lot of them seem to be related to a few root causes.

First, let's address the problem that, though the `Activity` and `Status` classes don't seem to have the `exclude` methods, some of our code tries to call that method. A typical report of this problem from the Nose output looks like a traceback followed by:

```
AttributeError: 'Activity' object has no attribute 'exclude'
```

Looking at our code, we see that it is properly called `excludes`. The tracebacks included in the Nose error report tell us that the problem is on line 51 of `planner/data.py`, and it looks like a quick fix.

We'll just change line 51 from the following:

```
if task.exclude(contained) or contained.exclude(task):
```

to:

```
if task.excludes(contained) or contained.excludes(task):
```

and run Nose again.

Similarly, several of our tests report the following output:

```
NameError: name 'containeed' is not defined
```

This is clearly another typo. That one's on line 52 of `planner/data.py`. Oops!! We'll fix that one, too, and run Nose again to see what else is wrong.

Continuing our trend of picking the low-hanging fruit first, let's clear up the problem reported as the following:

```
SyntaxError: unexpected EOF while parsing
```

This is yet another typo, this time in `docs/outline.txt`. This time, it's not a problem with the code being tested, but with the test itself. It still needs to be fixed.

The problem is that, when originally entering the tests, I apparently only typed in two dots at the beginning of several lines, instead of the three that tell doctest that an expression continues onto that line.

After fixing that, things are starting to get less obvious. Let's pick on this one next:

```
File "docs/outline.txt", line 36, in outline.txt
Failed example:
    duplicate_activity in schedule
Expected:
    True
Got:
    False
```

Why isn't the activity being seen as a member of the schedule? The previous example passed, which shows that the `in` operator works for the activity we actually added to the schedule. The failure shows up when we try to use an equivalent activity; once we realize that, we know what we need to fix. Either our `__eq__` method isn't working, or (as is the actual case) we forgot to write it.

We can fix this bug by adding the `__eq__` and `__ne__` methods to `Task`, which will be inherited by `Activity` and `Status`.

```
    def __eq__(self, other):
        return (self.name == other.name and
                self.begins == other.begins and
                self.ends == other.ends)

    def __ne__(self, other):
        return (self.name != other.name or
                self.begins != other.begins or
                self.ends != other.ends)
```

Now, two tasks that have the same name, start time, and end time will compare as equivalent even if one is a `Status` and the other is an `Activity`. The last isn't necessarily right, but it doesn't cause any of our tests to fail, so we'll leave it for now. If it becomes a problem later, we'll write a test that checks it, and then fix it.

What's the deal with this one?

```
File "docs/outline.txt", line 61, in outline.txt
Failed example:
    schedule.add(activity2)
Expected:
    Traceback (most recent call last):
    ScheduleError: "test activity 2" overlaps with "test activity 1"
Got:
    Traceback (most recent call last):
      File "/usr/lib64/python3.4/doctest.py", line 1324, in __run
        compileflags, 1), test.globs)
      File "<doctest outline.txt[20]>", line 1, in <module>
        schedule.add(activity2)
      File "planner/data.py", line 62, in add
        raise ScheduleError(task, contained)
    planner.data.ScheduleError: (<test activity 2 2014-06-01T10:15:00
2014-06-01T13:30:00>, <test activity 1 2014-06-01T09:05:00 2014-06-
01T12:30:00>)
```

Well, it looks ugly but, if you look at it, you'll see that `doctest` is just complaining that the raised exception doesn't print out as expected. It's even the right exception; it's just a question of formatting.

We can fix this on line 62 of `planner/data.py`, by changing the line to read:

```
raise ScheduleError('"{}" overlaps with "{}"'.format(task.name,
contained.name))
```

There's one more problem with this doctest example, which is that we wrote the name of the expected exception as `ScheduleError`, and that was how Python 2 printed out exceptions. Python 3 prints out exceptions with a qualified name, though, so we need to change it to `planner.data.ScheduleError` on line 63 of the doctest file.

Now, if you've been following along, all of the errors should be fixed, except for some of the acceptance tests in `docs/outline.txt`. Basically, these failing tests tell us that we haven't written the persistence code yet, which is true.

Try it for yourself – writing and debugging code

The basic procedure, as we've discussed before, is to write some code, then run the tests to find problems with the code, and repeat. When you happen to come across an error that isn't covered by an existing test, you need to write a new test and continue the process. Perform the following steps:

1. Write code that ought to satisfy at least some of your tests.

   Run your tests. If you've used the tools we talked about in the previous chapters, you should be able to run everything simply by executing:

   ```
   $ python3 -m nose
   ```

2. If there are errors in the code you've already written, use the test output to help you locate and identity them. Once you understand the bugs, try to fix them and then go back to step 2.
3. Once you've fixed all the errors in the code you've written, and if your project isn't complete, choose some new tests to concentrate on and go back to step 1.

Enough iterations on this procedure lead you to have a complete and tested project. Of course, the real task is more difficult than simply saying "it will work" but, in the end, it will work. You will produce a codebase that you can be confident in. It will also be an easier process than it would have been without the tests.

Your project might be done, but there's still more to do on the personal scheduler. At this stage of the chapter, I haven't finished going through the writing and debugging process. It's time to do that.

Writing the persistence tests

Since I don't have any actual unit tests for the persistence code yet, I'll start off by making some. In the process, I have to figure out how persistence will actually work. The following code goes in `tests/test_persistence.py`:

```
from unittest import TestCase
from planner.persistence import File

class test_file(TestCase):
    def test_basic(self):
        storage = File(':memory:')
        storage.store_object('tag1', ('some object',))
        self.assertEqual(tuple(storage.load_objects('tag1')),
                         (('some object',),))

    def test_multiple_tags(self):
        storage = File(':memory:')

        storage.store_object('tag1', 'A')
        storage.store_object('tag2', 'B')
        storage.store_object('tag1', 'C')
        storage.store_object('tag1', 'D')
        storage.store_object('tag3', 'E')
        storage.store_object('tag3', 'F')

        self.assertEqual(set(storage.load_objects('tag1')),
                         set(['A', 'C', 'D']))

        self.assertEqual(set(storage.load_objects('tag2')),
                         set(['B']))

        self.assertEqual(set(storage.load_objects('tag3')),
                         set(['E', 'F']))
```

Looking at each of the important sections of the test code, we see the following:

```
def test_basic(self):
    storage = File(':memory:')
    storage.store_object('tag1', ('some object',))
    self.assertEqual(tuple(storage.load_objects('tag1')),
                     (('some object',),))
```

The `test_basic` test creates `File`, stores a single object under the name `'tag1'`, and then loads that object back from storage and checks whether it is equal to the original object. It really is a very basic test, but it covers the simple use case.

> We don't need a test fixture here because we're not actually working with an on-disk file that we need to create and delete. The special filename `':memory:'` tells SQLite to do everything in memory. This is particularly handy for testing.

```
def test_multiple_tags(self):
    storage = File(':memory:')

    storage.store_object('tag1', 'A')
    storage.store_object('tag2', 'B')
    storage.store_object('tag1', 'C')
    storage.store_object('tag1', 'D')
    storage.store_object('tag3', 'E')
    storage.store_object('tag3', 'F')

    self.assertEqual(set(storage.load_objects('tag1')),
                     set(['A', 'C', 'D']))

    self.assertEqual(set(storage.load_objects('tag2')),
                     set(['B']))

    self.assertEqual(set(storage.load_objects('tag3')),
                     set(['E', 'F']))
```

The `test_multiple_tags` test creates a storage, and then stores multiple objects in it, some with duplicate tags. It then checks whether the storage keeps all of the objects with a given tag, and returns all of them on request.

In other words, all these tests define the persistence file as a multimap from string keys to object values.

> A multimap is a mapping between single keys and any number of values. In other words, each individual key might be associated with one value, of fifty.

Finishing up the personal planner

Now that there are at least basic unit tests covering the persistence mechanism, it's time to write the persistence code itself. The following goes in `planner/persistence.py`:

```
import sqlite3
from pickle import loads, dumps

class File:
    def __init__(self, path):
        self.connection = sqlite3.connect(path)

        try:
            self.connection.execute("""
                create table objects (tag, pickle)
            """)
        except sqlite3.OperationalError:
            pass

    def store_object(self, tag, object):
        self.connection.execute('insert into objects values (?, ?)',
                                (tag, dumps(object)))

    def load_objects(self, tag):
        cursor = self.connection.execute("""
                    select pickle from objects where tag like ?
                """, (tag,))
        return [loads(row['pickle']) for row in cursor]
```

The `store_object` method runs a short SQL statement to store the object into a database field. The object serialization is handled by the `dumps` function from the `pickle` module.

> The `pickle` module, as a whole, deals with storing and retrieving Python objects. The `dumps` function in particular transforms Python objects into byte strings that can be transformed back into a Python object via the `loads` function.

The `load_object` method uses SQL to query the database for the serialized version of every object stored under a given tag, and then uses `pickle.loads` to transform these serializations into real objects for it to return.

Now I run Nose to find out what's broken:

```
ERROR: test_multiple_tags (test_persistence.test_file)
----------------------------------------------------------------------
Traceback (most recent call last):
  File "tests/test_persistence.py", line 21, in test_multiple_tags
    self.assertEqual(set(storage.load_objects('tag1')),
  File "planner/persistence.py", line 23, in load_objects
    return [loads(row['pickle']) for row in cursor]
  File "planner/persistence.py", line 23, in <listcomp>
    return [loads(row['pickle']) for row in cursor]
TypeError: tuple indices must be integers, not str
```

Ah, yes. The `sqlite3` module returns the query rows as tuples, unless you tell it otherwise. I want to use column names as indexes, so I need to set the row factory. We'll add the following line to the `File` constructor:

```
self.connection.row_factory = sqlite3.Row
```

Now when I run Nose, the only problems it tells me about are that I haven't implemented `Schedule.load` and `Schedule.store` yet. Furthermore, there aren't any unit tests that check these methods. The only error comes from the specification doctest. It's time to write some more unit tests in `tests/test_schedules.py`:

```
class store_load_tests(TestCase):
    def setUp(self):
        fake_tasks = []
        for i in range(50):
            fake_task = Mock()
            fake_task.overlaps = Mock(return_value = False)
            fake_task.name = 'fake {}'.format(i)

        self.tasks = fake_tasks

    def tearDown(self):
        del self.tasks

    def test_store(self):
        fake_file = Mock()

        schedule = Schedule('test_schedule')

        for task in self.tasks:
```

```
            schedule.add(task)

        schedule.store(fake_file)

        for task in self.tasks:
            fake_file.store_object.assert_any_call('test_schedule',
task)

    def test_load(self):
        fake_file = Mock()

        fake_file.load_objects = Mock(return_value = self.tasks)

        schedule = Schedule.load(fake_file, 'test_schedule')

        fake_file.load_objects.assert_called_once_with('test_
schedule')

        self.assertEqual(set(schedule.tasks),
                         set(self.tasks))
```

Now that I have some tests to check against, it's time to write the store and load methods of the `Schedule` class in `planner/data.py`:

```
    def store(self, storage):
        for task in self.tasks:
            storage.store_object(self.name, task)

    @staticmethod
    def load(storage, name = 'schedule'):
        value = Schedule(name)

        for task in storage.load_objects(name):
            value.add(task)

        return value
```

These changes also imply a change to the Schedule constructor:

```
    def __init__(self, name = 'schedule'):
        self.tasks = []
        self.name = name
```

Okay, now, I run Nose, and... something's still broken::

```
File "docs/outline.txt", line 101, in outline.txt
Failed example:
    schedule == newsched
Expected:
    True
Got:
    False
```

Looks like schedules need to compare equal based on their contents, too. That's easily done:

```
    def __eq__(self, other):
        return self.tasks == other.tasks
```

Just like last time we wrote a comparison function; this one has some unusual behavior, in that it only considers two schedules equal if the tasks were added to them in the same order. Again, though this smells a little funny, it doesn't make any tests fail, and it's not clearly wrong; so we'll leave it until it matters.

Summary

In this chapter, we learned about how the skills that we covered in earlier parts of this book are applied in practice. We did this by stepping through a recording of your humble author's actual process in writing a package. At the same time, you had the chance to work through your own project, make your own decisions, and design your own tests. You've taken the lead in a test-driven project, and you should be able to do it again whenever you want.

Now that we've covered the heart of Python testing, we're ready to talk about testing at the integration and system levels, which we'll do in the next chapter.

8
Integration and System Testing

With all of the tools, techniques, and practices we've discussed so far, we've still only been been thinking about testing units: the smallest, meaningfully testable pieces of code. It's time to expand the focus, and start testing code that incorporates multiple units.

That means we need to:

- Think about what integration testing and system testing actually are
- Learn how to identify testable multi-unit segments of a program
- Use the tools we've learned in order to create tests for these segments

Introduction to integration testing and system testing

Integration testing is the process of checking whether the units of our program work together properly. At this stage, thanks to our unit tests, we can assume that each unit works as expected in isolation, and we're kicking the tests up to a new level of complexity. It's not practical to start the process with integration testing because, if the units don't work, the integration won't work either, and it will be harder to track down the problems. Once the units are solid, though, it's necessary to test that the things we build out of them also work. The interactions can be surprising.

While you're doing integration testing, you'll be putting the units together into bigger and bigger collections, and testing these collections. When your integration tests expand to cover the entirety of your program, they become system tests.

The trickiest part of integration testing is choosing which units to integrate into each test, so that you always have a solid base of code that you can believe in: a place to stand, while you pull in more code.

Deciding on an integration order

We're going to work through an exercise that will help you with the process of deciding where to put the boundaries of integration tests:

1. Using a piece of paper or a graphics program, write down names or representations for each of the units in the time planner project from *Chapter 7, Test-driven Development Walk-through*. Group the methods of each class together. Being part of the same class is an obvious relationship between units, and we'll take advantage of this. The `==` symbol here represents the Python `==` operator, which invokes the `__eq__` method on an object:

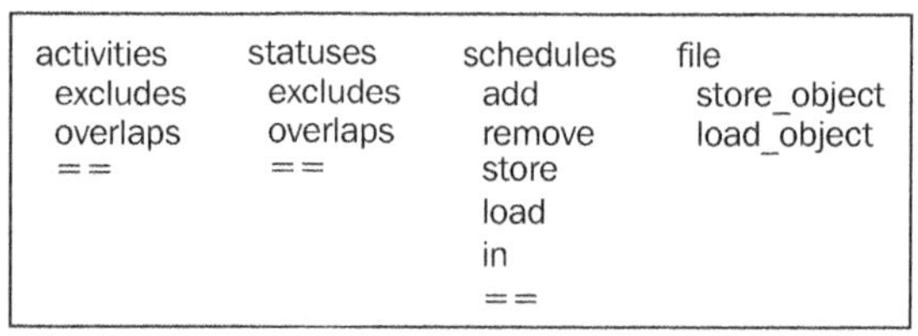

2. Now draw arrows between units that are supposed to directly interact with each other, from the caller to the callee. Laying everything out in an orderly fashion, as in step 1, can actually make this harder, so feel free to move the classes around to help the lines make sense:

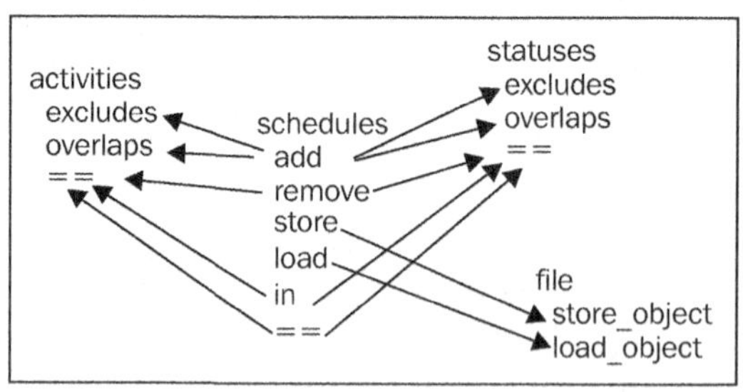

3. Draw circles around each class and each pair of classes connected by at least one line:

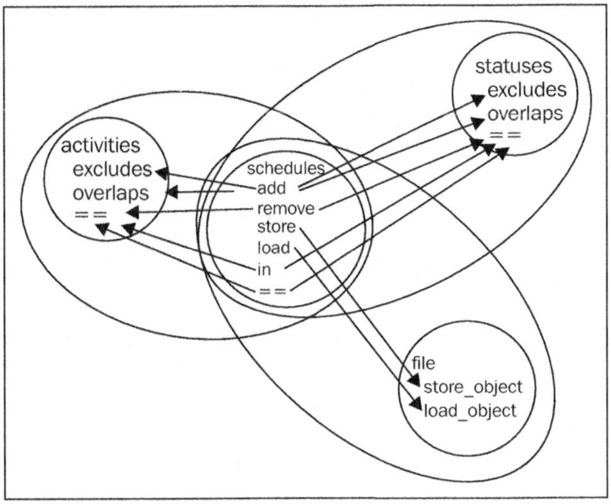

4. Continue the process by drawing circles around overlapping pairs of circles, until there are only three circles left. Circle a pair of them, and then put one more big circle around the whole mess:

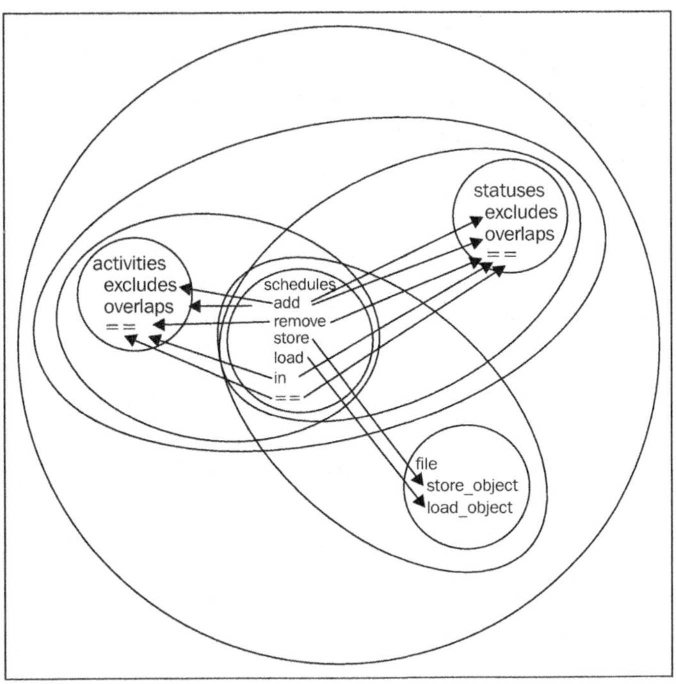

5. Now, to decide which integration tests to write first, we just have to look at the number of circles surrounding all parts of it. The more deeply nested the circle that contains every unit involved in an integration test is, the sooner we write that test.

What we just did is a way to visualize and solidify the process of building integration tests. While it's not critical to actually draw the lines and circles, it's useful to follow the process in your head. For larger projects, a lot can be gained from actually drawing the diagrams. When you see the diagram, the next correct step tends to jump right out at you—especially if you use multiple colors to render the diagram—where it might otherwise be hidden behind the complexity of the program.

Automating integration tests and system tests

The only real difference between an integration test and a unit test is that, in an integration test, you can break the code being tested into smaller meaningful chunks; in a unit test, however, if you divided the code any more, it wouldn't be meaningful. For this reason, the same tools that help you automate unit testing can be applied to integration testing. Since system testing is really the highest level of integration testing, the tools can be used for that as well.

The role of `doctest` in integration testing tends to be fairly limited: doctest's real strengths are in the early part of the development process. It's easy for a testable specification to stray into integration testing—as said before, that's fine as long as there are unit tests as well, but after that it's likely that you'll prefer `unittest` and Nose for writing your integration tests.

Integration tests need to be isolated from each other. Even though they contain multiple interacting units within themselves, you still benefit from knowing that nothing outside the test is affecting it. For this reason, `unittest` is a good choice for writing automated integration tests.

Writing integration tests for the time planner

The integration diagram only provides a partial ordering of the integration tests, and there are several tests that could be the first one we write. Looking at the diagram, we can see that the `Status` and `Activity` classes are at the end of a lot of arrows, but not at the beginning of any. This makes them particularly good places to start writing integration tests, because it means that they don't call on anything outside themselves to operate. Since there's nothing to distinguish one of them as a better place to start than the other, we can choose between them arbitrarily. Let's start with `Status`, and then do `Activity`. We're going to write tests that exercise the whole class. At this low level, the integration tests will look a lot like the unit tests for the same class, but we're not going to use mock objects to represent other instances of the same class. We will use real instances. We're testing whether the class correctly interacts with itself.

Here is the test code for `Status`:

```
from unittest import TestCase
from planner.data import Status
from datetime import datetime

class statuses_integration_tests(TestCase):
    def setUp(self):
        self.A = Status('A',
                        datetime(year = 2012, month = 7, day = 15),
                        datetime(year = 2013, month = 5, day = 2))

    def test_repr(self):
        self.assertEqual(repr(self.A), '<A 2012-07-15T00:00:00 2013-
05-02T00:00:00>')

    def test_equality(self):
        self.assertEqual(self.A, self.A)
        self.assertNotEqual(self.A, Status('B',
                          datetime(year = 2012, month = 7, day = 15),
                          datetime(year = 2013, month = 5, day = 2)))
        self.assertNotEqual(self.A, Status('A',
                          datetime(year = 2011, month = 7, day = 15),
                          datetime(year = 2013, month = 5, day = 2)))
        self.assertNotEqual(self.A, Status('A',
                          datetime(year = 2012, month = 7, day = 15),
                          datetime(year = 2014, month = 5, day = 2)))

    def test_overlap_begin(self):
        status = Status('status name',
                          datetime(year = 2011, month = 8, day = 11),
                          datetime(year = 2012, month = 11, day = 27))
```

```
            self.assertTrue(status.overlaps(self.A))

    def test_overlap_end(self):
        status = Status('status name',
                        datetime(year = 2012, month = 1, day = 11),
                        datetime(year = 2014, month = 4, day = 16))

        self.assertTrue(status.overlaps(self.A))

    def test_overlap_inner(self):
        status = Status('status name',
                        datetime(year = 2011, month = 10, day = 11),
                        datetime(year = 2014, month = 1, day = 27))

        self.assertTrue(status.overlaps(self.A))

    def test_overlap_outer(self):
        status = Status('status name',
                        datetime(year = 2012, month = 8, day = 12),
                        datetime(year = 2012, month = 9, day = 15))

        self.assertTrue(status.overlaps(self.A))

    def test_overlap_after(self):
        status = Status('status name',
                        datetime(year = 2015, month = 2, day = 6),
                        datetime(year = 2019, month = 4, day = 27))

        self.assertFalse(status.overlaps(self.A))
```

Here is the test code for `Activity`:

```
from unittest import TestCase
from planner.data import Activity, TaskError
from datetime import datetime

class activities_integration_tests(TestCase):
    def setUp(self):
        self.A = Activity('A',
                          datetime(year = 2012, month = 7, day = 15),
                          datetime(year = 2013, month = 5, day = 2))

    def test_repr(self):
        self.assertEqual(repr(self.A), '<A 2012-07-15T00:00:00 2013-
05-02T00:00:00>')

    def test_equality(self):
        self.assertEqual(self.A, self.A)
```

```
        self.assertNotEqual(self.A, Activity('B',
                            datetime(year = 2012, month = 7, day = 15),
                            datetime(year = 2013, month = 5, day = 2)))
        self.assertNotEqual(self.A, Activity('A',
                            datetime(year = 2011, month = 7, day = 15),
                            datetime(year = 2013, month = 5, day = 2)))
        self.assertNotEqual(self.A, Activity('A',
                            datetime(year = 2012, month = 7, day = 15),
                            datetime(year = 2014, month = 5, day = 2)))

    def test_overlap_begin(self):
        activity = Activity('activity name',
                            datetime(year = 2011, month = 8, day = 11),
                            datetime(year = 2012, month = 11, day = 27))

        self.assertTrue(activity.overlaps(self.A))
        self.assertTrue(activity.excludes(self.A))

    def test_overlap_end(self):
        activity = Activity('activity name',
                            datetime(year = 2012, month = 1, day = 11),
                            datetime(year = 2014, month = 4, day = 16))

        self.assertTrue(activity.overlaps(self.A))
        self.assertTrue(activity.excludes(self.A))

    def test_overlap_inner(self):
        activity = Activity('activity name',
                            datetime(year = 2011, month = 10, day = 11),
                            datetime(year = 2014, month = 1, day = 27))

        self.assertTrue(activity.overlaps(self.A))
        self.assertTrue(activity.excludes(self.A))

    def test_overlap_outer(self):
        activity = Activity('activity name',
                            datetime(year = 2012, month = 8, day = 12),
                            datetime(year = 2012, month = 9, day = 15))

        self.assertTrue(activity.overlaps(self.A))
        self.assertTrue(activity.excludes(self.A))

    def test_overlap_after(self):
        activity = Activity('activity name',
                            datetime(year = 2015, month = 2, day = 6),
                            datetime(year = 2019, month = 4, day = 27))

        self.assertFalse(activity.overlaps(self.A))
```

Looking at our diagram, we can see that the next level out from either `Status` or `Activity` represents the integration of these classes with the `Schedule` class. Before we write this integration, we ought to write any tests that involve the `Schedule` class interacting with itself, without using mock objects:

```
from unittest import TestCase
from unittest.mock import Mock
from planner.data import Schedule
from datetime import datetime

class schedule_tests(TestCase):
    def test_equality(self):
        A = Mock(overlaps = Mock(return_value = False))
        B = Mock(overlaps = Mock(return_value = False))
        C = Mock(overlaps = Mock(return_value = False))

        sched1 = Schedule()
        sched2 = Schedule()

        self.assertEqual(sched1, sched2)

        sched1.add(A)
        sched1.add(B)

        sched2.add(A)
        sched2.add(B)
        sched2.add(C)

        self.assertNotEqual(sched1, sched2)

        sched1.add(C)

        self.assertEqual(sched1, sched2)
```

Now that the interactions within the `Schedule` class have been tested, we can write tests that integrate `Schedule` with either `Status` or `Activity`. Let's start with `Status`, then do `Activity`.

Here are the tests for `Schedule` and `Status`:

```
from planner.data import Schedule, Status
from unittest import TestCase
from datetime import datetime, timedelta
```

```
class test_schedules_and_statuses(TestCase):
    def setUp(self):
        self.A = Status('A',
                        datetime.now(),
                        datetime.now() + timedelta(minutes = 7))
        self.B = Status('B',
                        datetime.now() - timedelta(hours = 1),
                        datetime.now() + timedelta(hours = 1))
        self.C = Status('C',
                        datetime.now() + timedelta(minutes = 10),
                        datetime.now() + timedelta(hours = 1))

    def test_usage_pattern(self):
        sched = Schedule()

        sched.add(self.A)
        sched.add(self.C)

        self.assertTrue(self.A in sched)
        self.assertTrue(self.C in sched)
        self.assertFalse(self.B in sched)

        sched.add(self.B)

        self.assertTrue(self.B in sched)

        self.assertEqual(sched, sched)

        sched.remove(self.A)

        self.assertFalse(self.A in sched)
        self.assertTrue(self.B in sched)
        self.assertTrue(self.C in sched)

        sched.remove(self.B)
        sched.remove(self.C)

        self.assertFalse(self.B in sched)
        self.assertFalse(self.C in sched)
```

Here are the tests for the interactions between real `Schedule` and `Activity` instances. Due to the similarity between `Activity` and `Status`, the tests are, not surprisingly, structured similarly:

```
from planner.data import Schedule, Activity, ScheduleError
from unittest import TestCase
from datetime import datetime, timedelta

class test_schedules_and_activities(TestCase):
    def setUp(self):
        self.A = Activity('A',
                          datetime.now(),
                          datetime.now() + timedelta(minutes = 7))
        self.B = Activity('B',
                          datetime.now() - timedelta(hours = 1),
                          datetime.now() + timedelta(hours = 1))
        self.C = Activity('C',
                          datetime.now() + timedelta(minutes = 10),
                          datetime.now() + timedelta(hours = 1))

    def test_usage_pattern(self):
        sched = Schedule()

        sched.add(self.A)
        sched.add(self.C)

        self.assertTrue(self.A in sched)
        self.assertTrue(self.C in sched)
        self.assertFalse(self.B in sched)

        self.assertRaises(ScheduleError, sched.add, self.B)

        self.assertFalse(self.B in sched)

        self.assertEqual(sched, sched)

        sched.remove(self.A)

        self.assertFalse(self.A in sched)
        self.assertFalse(self.B in sched)
        self.assertTrue(self.C in sched)

        sched.remove(self.C)

        self.assertFalse(self.B in sched)
        self.assertFalse(self.C in sched)
```

All right, it's finally time to put `Schedule`, `Status`, and `Activity` together in the same test:

```
from planner.data import Schedule, Status, Activity, ScheduleError
from unittest import TestCase
from datetime import datetime, timedelta

class test_schedules_activities_and_statuses(TestCase):
    def setUp(self):
        self.A = Status('A',
                        datetime.now(),
                        datetime.now() + timedelta(minutes = 7))
        self.B = Status('B',
                        datetime.now() - timedelta(hours = 1),
                        datetime.now() + timedelta(hours = 1))
        self.C = Status('C',
                        datetime.now() + timedelta(minutes = 10),
                        datetime.now() + timedelta(hours = 1))

        self.D = Activity('D',
                          datetime.now(),
                          datetime.now() + timedelta(minutes = 7))

        self.E = Activity('E',
                          datetime.now() + timedelta(minutes = 30),
                          datetime.now() + timedelta(hours = 1))

        self.F = Activity('F',
                          datetime.now() - timedelta(minutes = 20),
                          datetime.now() + timedelta(minutes = 40))

    def test_usage_pattern(self):
        sched = Schedule()

        sched.add(self.A)
        sched.add(self.B)
        sched.add(self.C)

        sched.add(self.D)

        self.assertTrue(self.A in sched)
        self.assertTrue(self.B in sched)
        self.assertTrue(self.C in sched)
        self.assertTrue(self.D in sched)

        self.assertRaises(ScheduleError, sched.add, self.F)
        self.assertFalse(self.F in sched)
```

```
        sched.add(self.E)
        sched.remove(self.D)

        self.assertTrue(self.E in sched)
        self.assertFalse(self.D in sched)

        self.assertRaises(ScheduleError, sched.add, self.F)

        self.assertFalse(self.F in sched)

        sched.remove(self.E)

        self.assertFalse(self.E in sched)

        sched.add(self.F)

        self.assertTrue(self.F in sched)
```

The next thing we need to pull in is the `File` class but, before we integrate it with the rest of the system, we need to integrate it with itself and check its internal interactions without using mock objects:

```
from unittest import TestCase
from planner.persistence import File
from os import unlink

class test_file(TestCase):
    def setUp(self):
        storage = File('file_test.sqlite')

        storage.store_object('tag1', 'A')
        storage.store_object('tag2', 'B')
        storage.store_object('tag1', 'C')
        storage.store_object('tag1', 'D')
        storage.store_object('tag3', 'E')
        storage.store_object('tag3', 'F')

    def tearDown(self):
        try:
            unlink('file_test.sqlite')
        except OSError:
            pass

    def test_other_instance(self):
        storage = File('file_test.sqlite')
```

```
        self.assertEqual(set(storage.load_objects('tag1')),
                         set(['A', 'C', 'D']))

        self.assertEqual(set(storage.load_objects('tag2')),
                         set(['B']))

        self.assertEqual(set(storage.load_objects('tag3')),
                         set(['E', 'F']))
```

Now we can write tests that integrate `Schedules` and `File`. Notice that, for this step, we still aren't involving `Status` or `Activity`, because they're outside the oval. We'll use mock objects in place of them, for now:

```
from unittest import TestCase
from unittest.mock import Mock
from planner.data import Schedule
from planner.persistence import File
from os import unlink

def unpickle_mocked_task(begins):
    return Mock(overlaps = Mock(return_value = False), begins =
begins)

class test_schedules_and_file(TestCase):
    def setUp(self):
        A = Mock(overlaps = Mock(return_value = False),
                 __reduce__ = Mock(return_value = (unpickle_mocked_
task, (5,))),
                 begins = 5)

        B = Mock(overlaps = Mock(return_value = False),
                 __reduce__ = Mock(return_value = (unpickle_mocked_
task, (3,))),
                 begins = 3)

        C = Mock(overlaps = Mock(return_value = False),
                 __reduce__ = Mock(return_value = (unpickle_mocked_
task, (7,))),
                 begins = 7)

        self.A = A
        self.B = B
        self.C = C
```

```
    def tearDown(self):
        try:
            unlink('test_schedules_and_file.sqlite')
        except OSError:
            pass

    def test_save_and_restore(self):
        sched1 = Schedule()

        sched1.add(self.A)
        sched1.add(self.B)
        sched1.add(self.C)

        store1 = File('test_schedules_and_file.sqlite')
        sched1.store(store1)

        del sched1
        del store1

        store2 = File('test_schedules_and_file.sqlite')
        sched2 = Schedule.load(store2)

        self.assertEqual(set([x.begins for x in sched2.tasks]),
                         set([3, 5, 7]))
```

We've built our way up to the outermost circle now, which means it's time to write tests that involve the whole system with no mock objects anywhere:

```
from planner.data import Schedule, Status, Activity, ScheduleError
from planner.persistence import File
from unittest import TestCase
from datetime import datetime, timedelta
from os import unlink

class test_system(TestCase):
    def setUp(self):
        self.A = Status('A',
                        datetime.now(),
                        datetime.now() + timedelta(minutes = 7))
        self.B = Status('B',
                        datetime.now() - timedelta(hours = 1),
                        datetime.now() + timedelta(hours = 1))
        self.C = Status('C',
                        datetime.now() + timedelta(minutes = 10),
                        datetime.now() + timedelta(hours = 1))
```

```
        self.D = Activity('D',
                          datetime.now(),
                          datetime.now() + timedelta(minutes = 7))

        self.E = Activity('E',
                          datetime.now() + timedelta(minutes = 30),
                          datetime.now() + timedelta(hours = 1))

        self.F = Activity('F',
                          datetime.now() - timedelta(minutes = 20),
                          datetime.now() + timedelta(minutes = 40))

    def tearDown(self):
        try:
            unlink('test_system.sqlite')
        except OSError:
            pass

    def test_usage_pattern(self):
        sched1 = Schedule()

        sched1.add(self.A)
        sched1.add(self.B)
        sched1.add(self.C)
        sched1.add(self.D)
        sched1.add(self.E)

        store1 = File('test_system.sqlite')
        sched1.store(store1)

        del store1

        store2 = File('test_system.sqlite')
        sched2 = Schedule.load(store2)

        self.assertEqual(sched1, sched2)

        sched2.remove(self.D)
        sched2.remove(self.E)

        self.assertNotEqual(sched1, sched2)

        sched2.add(self.F)

        self.assertTrue(self.F in sched2)
        self.assertFalse(self.F in sched1)
```

```
        self.assertRaises(ScheduleError, sched2.add, self.D)
        self.assertRaises(ScheduleError, sched2.add, self.E)

        self.assertTrue(self.A in sched1)
        self.assertTrue(self.B in sched1)
        self.assertTrue(self.C in sched1)
        self.assertTrue(self.D in sched1)
        self.assertTrue(self.E in sched1)
        self.assertFalse(self.F in sched1)

        self.assertTrue(self.A in sched2)
        self.assertTrue(self.B in sched2)
        self.assertTrue(self.C in sched2)
        self.assertFalse(self.D in sched2)
        self.assertFalse(self.E in sched2)
        self.assertTrue(self.F in sched2)
```

We've just integrated our whole code base, progressively constructing larger tests until we had tests encompassing the whole system. The whole time, we were careful to test one thing at a time. Because we took care to go step-by-step, we always knew where the newly discovered bugs originated, and we were able to fix them easily.

Speaking of which, if you were to run the tests for yourself while building this code structure, you would notice that some of them fail. All three of the failures point to the same problem: there's something wrong with the persistence database. This error doesn't show up in the unit tests for the `File` class, because it's only visible on a larger scale, when the database is used to communicate information between units.

Here's the error reported by the `test_file.py` tests:

```
Traceback (most recent call last):
  File "integration/integration_tests/test_file.py", line 26, in test_other_instance
    set(['A', 'C', 'D']))
AssertionError: Items in the second set but not the first:
'A'
'D'
'C'
```

The changes to the database aren't being committed to the file, and so they aren't visible outside the transaction where they were stored. Not testing the persistence code in separate transactions was not an oversight, but that's exactly the sort of mistake that we expect integration testing to catch.

We can fix the problem by altering the `store_object` method of the `File` class in `persistence.py` as follows:

```
def store_object(self, tag, object):
    self.connection.execute('insert into objects values (?, ?)',
                            (tag, dumps(object)))
    self.connection.commit()
```

Another point of interest is the interaction between `pickle` and mock objects. There are a lot of things that mock objects do well, but accepting pickling is not one of them. Fortunately, that's relatively easy to work around is demonstrated in test integrating `Schedule` and `File`:

```
def unpickle_mocked_task(begins):
    return Mock(overlaps = Mock(return_value = False), begins =
begins)

class test_schedules_and_file(TestCase):
    def setUp(self):
        A = Mock(overlaps = Mock(return_value = False),
                 __reduce__ = Mock(return_value = (unpickle_mocked_
task, (5,))),
                 begins = 5)

        B = Mock(overlaps = Mock(return_value = False),
                 __reduce__ = Mock(return_value = (unpickle_mocked_
task, (3,))),
                 begins = 3)

        C = Mock(overlaps = Mock(return_value = False),
                 __reduce__ = Mock(return_value = (unpickle_mocked_
task, (7,))),
                 begins = 7)
```

The trick here is not really very tricky. We've just told the mock objects what return value to use for calls to the `__reduce__` method. It so happens that the pickle dumping functions call `__reduce__` to find out whether an object needs special handling when being pickled and unpickled. We told it that it did, and that it should call the `unpickle_mocked_task` function to reconstitute the mock object during unpickling. Now, our mock objects can be pickled and unpickled as well as the real objects can.

Another point of interest in the tests for `Schedule` and `File` is the `tearDown` test fixture method. The `tearDown` method will delete a database file, if it exists, but won't complain if it doesn't. The database is expected to be created within the test itself, and we don't want to leave it lying around; however, if it's not there, it's not a test fixture error:

```
def tearDown(self):
    try:
        unlink('test_schedules_and_file.sqlite')
    except OSError:
        pass
```

A lot of the test code in this chapter might seem redundant to you. That's because, in some sense, it is. Some things are repeatedly checked in different tests. Why bother?

The main reason for the redundancy is that each test is supposed to stand alone. We're not supposed to care what order they run in, or whether any other tests even exist. Each test is self-contained; thus, if it fails, we know exactly what needs to be fixed. Because each test is self-contained, some foundational things end up getting tested multiple times. In the case of this simple project, redundancy is even more pronounced than it would normally be.

Whether it's blatant or subtle, though, the redundancy isn't a problem. The so-called **Don't Repeat Yourself** (**DRY**) principle doesn't particularly apply to tests. There's not much downside to having something tested multiple times. This is not to say that it's a good idea to copy and paste tests, because it's very much not. Don't be surprised or alarmed to see similarities between your tests, but don't use that as an excuse. Every test that checks a particular thing is a test that needs to be changed if you change that thing, so it's still best to minimize redundancy where you can.

Check yourself – writing integration tests

Try answering the following questions to check about integration tests yourself:

1. Which integration tests do you write first?

   Answer: The ones in the smallest circles, especially if they don't have any lines pointing from themselves to other circles. Put another way, write the most independent tests first.

2. What happens when you have a large chunk of integrated code, but the next section you need to pull in doesn't have any integration tests at all?

   Answer: Start from the smallest circles involving that code, and build up step-by-step until you're ready to integrate it with your earlier code.

3. What's the point of writing tests that check the integration of a chunk of code with itself?

   Answer: When we were doing unit testing, even other instances of the same class were mocked, as were other methods of the same instance when it was reasonable to do so; we were concerned that this code did what it was supposed to, without involving anything else. Now that we're doing integration testing, we need to test the instances of the same class that interact correctly with each other, or with themselves when they're allowed to retain a state from one operation to the next. The two kinds of tests cover different things, so it makes sense that we would need both.

4. What is a system test and how do system tests relate to integration tests?

   Answer: A system test is the final stage of integration testing. It's a test that involves the whole code base.

Summary

In this chapter, we learned about the process of building from a foundation of unit tests into a set of tests that cover the whole system.

Specifically, we covered how to draw an integration diagram. We learned how to interpret an integration diagram to decide in what order to build the tests and also learned which tools to use and how to use them to write the integration tests.

Now that we've learned about integration testing, we're ready to introduce a number of other useful testing tools and strategies, which is the topic of the next chapter.

9
Other Tools and Techniques

We've covered the core elements of testing in Python, but there are a number of peripheral methods and tools that will make your life easier. In this chapter, we're going to go through several of them in brief.

In this chapter, we're going to:

- Discuss code coverage and how to get a code coverage report from Nose
- Discuss continuous integration and Buildbot
- Learn how to integrate automated testing with Git, Mercurial, Bazaar, and Subversion

Code coverage

Tests tell you when the code you're testing doesn't work the way you thought it would, but they don't tell you a thing about the code you're not testing. They don't even tell you that the code you're not testing isn't being tested.

Code coverage is a technique to address that shortcoming. A code coverage tool watches while your tests are running, and keeps track of which lines of code are (and aren't) executed. After the tests have run, the tool will give you a report describing how well your tests cover the whole body of code.

It's desirable to have the coverage approach 100 percent, as you probably figured out already. Be careful not to focus on the coverage number too intensely, though, because it can be a bit misleading. Even if your tests execute every line of code in the program, they can easily not test everything that needs to be tested. This means that you can't take 100 percent coverage as certain proof that your tests are complete. On the other hand, there are times when some code really, truly doesn't need to be covered by the tests—some debugging support code, for example, or code generated by a user interface builder—and so less than 100 percent coverage is often completely acceptable.

Code coverage is a tool to give you an insight into what your tests are doing, and what they might be overlooking. It's not the definition of a good test suite.

Installing coverage.py

We're going to be working with a module called `coverage.py`, which is—unsurprisingly—a code coverage tool for Python.

Since `coverage.py` isn't built in to Python, we're going to need to download and install it. You can download the latest version from the Python Package Index at `http://pypi.python.org/pypi/coverage`, but it will probably be easier simply to type the following from the command line:

```
python3 -m pip install --user coverage
```

We're going to walk through the steps of using `coverage.py` here, but if you want more information you can find it on the `coverage.py` home page at `http://nedbatchelder.com/code/coverage/`.

Using coverage.py with Nose

We're going to create a little toy code module with tests, and then apply `coverage.py` to find out how much of the code the tests actually use.

Put the following test code into `test_toy.py`. There are several problems with these tests, which we'll discuss later, but they ought to run:

```
from unittest import TestCase
import toy

class test_global_function(TestCase):
    def test_positive(self):
        self.assertEqual(toy.global_function(3), 4)

    def test_negative(self):
        self.assertEqual(toy.global_function(-3), -2)

    def test_large(self):
        self.assertEqual(toy.global_function(2**13), 2**13 + 1)

class test_example_class(TestCase):
    def test_timestwo(self):
        example = toy.Example(5)
        self.assertEqual(example.timestwo(), 10)
```

What we have here is a couple of `TestCase` classes with some very basic tests in them. These tests wouldn't be of much use in a real-world situation, but all we need them for is to illustrate how the code coverage tool works.

Put the following code into `toy.py`. Notice the `if __name__ == '__main__'` clause at the bottom; we haven't dealt with one of these in a while, so I'll remind you that the code inside that block runs `doctest` if we were to run the module with Python `toy.py`:

```
def global_function(x):
    r"""
    >>> global_function(5)
    6
    """
    return x + 1

class Example:
    def __init__(self, param):
        self.param = param

    def timestwo(self):
        return self.param * 2

    def __repr__(self):
        return 'Example({!r})'.format(self.param)

if __name__ == '__main__':
    import doctest
    doctest.testmod()
```

Here, we have the code that satisfies the tests we just wrote. Like the tests themselves, this code wouldn't be of much use, but it serves as an illustration.

Go ahead and run Nose. It should find the tests, run them, and report that all is well. The problem is that some of the code isn't ever tested. Let's run the tests again, only this time we'll tell Nose to use `coverage.py` to measure coverage while it's running the tests:

```
python -m nose --with-coverage --cover-erase
```

This should give us an error report that looks like this:

```
.....
Name     Stmts    Miss   Cover    Missing
-------------------------------------
```

```
toy          12       3     75%    16, 19-20
-------------------------------------------------------------------
Ran 5 tests in 0.053s

OK
```

The dots at the top indicate passing tests, and the `OK` at the bottom says that the testing procedure worked as expected, but the part in between is new. That's our coverage report. Apparently, our tests only cover three quarters of our code: out of the 12 statement lines in `toy.py`, three didn't get executed. These lines were `16` and `19` through `20`.

> The range `19-20` isn't any more useful than writing `19, 20` would have been, but larger contiguous groups of lines are reported in the same way. That's a lot easier to parse, visually, than a soup of separate line numbers would be, especially when it's a range like `361-947`.

When we passed `--with-coverage` and `--cover-erase` as command-line parameters to Nose, what did they do? Well, `--with-coverage` is pretty straightforward: it told Nose to look for `coverage.py` and to use it while the tests get executed. That's just what we wanted. The second parameter, `--cover-erase`, tells Nose to forget about any coverage information that was acquired during previous runs. By default, coverage information is aggregated across all of the uses of `coverage.py`. This allows you to run a set of tests using different testing frameworks or mechanisms, and then check the cumulative coverage. You still want to erase the data from previous test runs at the beginning of this process, though, and the `--cover-erase` command line is how you tell Nose to tell `coverage.py` that you're starting a new.

> Nose, being an integrated testing system, often renders the need to aggregate coverage information that is negligible. You'll almost always want `--cover-erase` when you invoke Nose with coverage enabled, so you should consider adding `cover-erase=1` to your Nose configuration file, as discussed in previous chapters.

Another useful Nose command-line option is `--cover-package=PACKAGE`, which limits the coverage report to the specific package you're interested in. It didn't show up in our toy because we didn't import anything, but normally the coverage report includes every module or package that has code executed while your tests are running. The percentage of the standard library that is covered by your tests is usually not useful information. It can be convenient to limit the report to the things you actually want to know.

So, back to our coverage report. The missing lines were line `16` and lines `19` through `20`. Looking back at our code, we see that line `16` is the `__repr__` method. We really should have tested that, so the coverage check has revealed a hole in our tests that we should fix. Lines `19` and `20` are just code to run `doctest`, though. They're not something that we ought to be using under production conditions, so we can just ignore that coverage hole.

Code coverage can't detect problems with the tests themselves, in most cases. In the previous test code, the test for the `timestwo` method violates the isolation of units and invokes two different methods of `example_class`. Since one of the methods is the constructor, this might be acceptable, but the coverage checker isn't in a position to even see that there might be a problem. All it saw was more lines of code being covered. That's not a problem—it's how a coverage checker ought to work—but it's something to keep in mind. Coverage is useful, but high coverage doesn't equal good tests.

Version control integration

Most version control systems have the ability to run a program you've written in response to various events, as a way of customizing the version control system's behavior. These programs are commonly called **hooks**.

You can do all kinds of things by installing the right hook programs, but we're only going to focus on one use. We can make the version control program automatically run our tests, when we commit a new version of the code to the version control repository.

This is a fairly nifty trick, because this makes it difficult for test-breaking bugs to get into the repository unnoticed. Somewhat like code coverage, though, there's potential for trouble if it becomes a matter of policy rather than simply being a tool to make your life easier.

In most systems, you can write the hooks so that it's impossible to commit code that breaks tests. This might sound like a good idea at first, but it's really not. One reason for this is that one of the major purposes of a version control system is communication between developers, and interfering with that tends to be unproductive in the long run. Another reason is that it prevents anybody from committing partial solutions to problems, which means that things tend to get dumped into the repository in big chunks. Big commits are a problem because they make it hard to keep track of what changed, which adds to the confusion. There are better ways to make sure that you always have a working code base socked away somewhere, such as version control branches.

Git

Git has become the most widely used distributed version control system, so we'll start there. By virtue of its being distributed, and thus decentralized, each Git user can control their own hooks. Cloning a repository will not clone the hooks for that repository.

If you don't have Git installed and don't plan to use it, you can skip this section.

Git hooks are stored in the `.git/hooks/` subdirectory of the repository, each in its own file. The ones that we're interested in are the `pre-commit` hook and the `prepare-commit-msg` hook, either of which would potentially be suitable to our purposes.

All Git hooks are programs that Git executes automatically at a specific time. If a program named `pre-commit` exists in the `hooks` directory, it is run before a commit happens to check whether the commit is valid. If a program named `prepare-commit-msg` exists in the `hooks` directory, it is run to modify the default commit message that is presented to the user.

So, the `pre-commit` hook is the one we want if we want the failed tests to abort the commit (which is acceptable with Git, though I still don't recommend it because there's a command-line option, `--no-verify`, that allows the user to commit even if the tests fail). We can also run the tests from `pre-commit` and print the error report to the screen, while allowing the commit, regardless of the result, by simply producing a zero result code after we invoke Nose, instead of passing on the Nose result code.

If we want to get fancier and add the test report to the commit message, or include it in the commit message file that will be shown to the user without actually adding it to the commit message, we need the `prepare-commit-msg` hook instead. This is what we're going to do in our example.

Example test-runner hook

As I mentioned, Git hooks are programs, which means that we can write them in Python. If you place the following code in a file named `.git/hooks/prepare-commit-msg` (and make it executable) within one of your Git repositories, your Nose test suite will be run before each commit, and the test report will be presented to you when you are prompted for a commit message, but commented out so as to not actually end up in the Git log. If the tests convince you that you don't want to commit yet, all you have to do is leave the message blank to abort the commit.

> In Windows, a file named `prepare-commit-msg` won't be executable. You'll need to name the actual hook program `prepare-commit-msg.py` and create a batch file named `prepare-commit-msg.bat` containing the following (assuming you have Python's program directory in the `PATH` environment variable):
>
> ```
> @echo off
> pythonw prepare-commit-msg.py
> ```
>
> This is the first time I've mentioned the `pythonw` command. It's a Windows-specific version of the Python interpreter with only one difference from the normal Python program: it does not open a terminal window for text-mode interactions. When a program is run via `pythonw` on Windows, nothing is visible to the user unless the program intentionally creates a user interface.

So, without further ado, here is the Python program for a Git `prepare-commit-msg` hook that integrates Nose:

```
#!/usr/bin/env python3
from sys import argv
from subprocess import check_output, CalledProcessError, STDOUT

PYTHON = ['pythonw', 'python']
NOSE = ['-m', 'nose', '--with-coverage', '--cover-erase']

lines = ['', '# Nose test report:']

report = None

try:
    for command in PYTHON:
        try:
            report = check_output([command] + NOSE,
                                  stderr=STDOUT,
                                  universal_newlines=True)
        except FileNotFoundError:
            pass
        else:
            break
except CalledProcessError as x:
    report = x.output
```

```
if report is None:
    lines.append('#    Unable to run Python.')
else:
    for line in report.splitlines():
        if not line:
            lines.append('')
        else:
            lines.append('# ' + line)

with open(argv[1], 'r') as f:
    lines.append(f.read())

with open(argv[1], 'w') as f:
    f.write('\n'.join(lines))
```

Now, whenever you run a Git `commit` command, you'll get a Nose report:

```
git commit -a
```

Subversion

Subversion is the most popular freely available centralized version control system. There is a single server tasked with keeping track of everybody's changes, and this server also handles running hooks. This means that there is a single set of hooks that applies to everybody, probably under the control of a system administrator.

If you don't have Subversion installed and don't plan on using it, you can skip this section.

Subversion hooks are stored in files in the `hooks` subdirectory of the server's repository. Because Subversion operates on a centralized, client-server architecture, we're going to need both a client and a server setup for this example. They can both be on the same computer, but they'll be in different directories.

Before we can work with concrete examples, we need a Subversion server. You can create one by making a new directory called `svnrepo`, and executing the following command:

```
$ svnadmin create svnrepo/
```

Now, we need to configure the server to accept commits from us. To do this, we open the file called `conf/passwd`, and add the following line at the bottom:

```
testuser = testpass
```

Then we need to edit `conf/svnserve.conf`, and change the line reading:

```
# password-db = passwd
```

into the following:

```
password-db = passwd
```

The Subversion server needs to be running before we can interact with it. This is done by making sure that we're in the `svnrepo` directory and then run the command:

```
svnserve -d -r ..
```

Next, we need to import some test code into the Subversion repository. Make a directory and place the following (simple and silly) code into it in a file called `test_simple.py`:

```
from unittest import TestCase

class test_simple(TestCase):
    def test_one(self):
        self.assertNotEqual("Testing", "Hooks")

    def test_two(self):
        self.assertEqual("Same", "Same")
```

You can perform the import by executing the following command:

```
$ svn import --username=testuser --password=testpass svn://localhost/
svnrepo/
```

> Subversion needs to know which text editor you want to use. If the preceding command fails, you probably need to tell it explicitly. You can do this by setting the `SVN_EDITOR` environment variable to the program path of the editor you prefer.

That command is likely to print out a gigantic, scary message about remembering passwords. In spite of the warnings, just say yes.

Now that we've got the code imported, we need to check out a copy of it to work on. We can do this with the following command:

```
$ svn checkout --username=testuser --password=testpass svn://localhost/
svnrepo/ svn
```

> From here on, in this example, we're going to be assuming that the Subversion server is running in a Unix-like environment (the clients might be running on Windows, but that doesn't matter for our purposes). The reason for this is that the details of the `post-commit` hook are significantly different on systems that don't have a Unix style shell scripting language, although the concepts remain the same.

The following code goes into a file called `hooks/post-commit` inside the Subversion server's repository. The `svn update` and `svn checkout` lines have been wrapped around to fit on the page. In actual use, this wrapping should not be present:

```
#!/bin/sh
REPO="$1"

if /usr/bin/test -e "$REPO/working"; then
    /usr/bin/svn update --username=testuser --password=testpass
"$REPO/working/";
else
    /usr/bin/svn checkout --username=testuser --password=testpass
svn://localhost/svnrepo/ "$REPO/working/";
fi

cd "$REPO/working/"

exec /usr/bin/nosetests
```

Use the `chmod +x post-commit` command to make the hook executable.

Change to the `svn` checkout directory and edit `test_simple.py` to make one of the tests fail. We do this because, if all the tests pass, Subversion won't show us anything to indicate that they were run at all. We only get feedback if they fail:

```
from unittest import TestCase

class test_simple(TestCase):
    def test_one(self):
        self.assertNotEqual("Testing", "Hooks")

    def test_two(self):
        self.assertEqual("Same", "Same!")
```

Now commit the changes using the following command:

```
$ svn commit --username=testuser --password=testpass
```

Notice that the commit triggered the execution of Nose, and that, if any of the tests fail, Subversion shows us the errors.

Because Subversion has one central set of hooks, they can be applied automatically to anybody who uses the repository.

Mercurial

Like Git, Mercurial is a distributed version control system with hooks that are managed by each user individually. Mercurial's hooks themselves, though, take a rather different form.

If you don't have Mercurial installed and don't plan to use it, you can skip this section.

Mercurial hooks can go in several different places. The two most useful are in your personal configuration file and in your repository configuration file.

Your personal configuration file is `~/.hgrc` on Unix-like systems, and `%USERPROFILE%\Mercurial.ini` (which usually means `C:\Documents and Settings\<username>\Mercurial.ini`) on Windows-based systems.

Your repository configuration file is stored in a subdirectory of the repository, specifically, `.hg/hgrc`, on all systems.

We're going to use the repository configuration file to store the hook, which means that the first thing we have to do is have a repository to work with. Make a new directory somewhere convenient, and execute the following command in it:

```
$ hg init
```

One side-effect of this command is that a `.hg` subdirectory gets created. Change to this directory, and then create a text file called `hgrc` containing the following text:

```
[hooks]
commit = python3 -m nose
```

In the repository directory (that is, the parent of the `.hg` directory), we need some tests for Nose to run. Create a file called `test_simple.py` containing the following, admittedly silly, tests:

```
from unittest import TestCase

class test_simple(TestCase):
    def test_one(self):
        self.assertNotEqual("Testing", "Hooks")

    def test_two(self):
        self.assertEqual("Same", "Same")
```

Run the following commands to add the test file and commit it to the repository:

```
$ hg add
$ hg commit
```

Notice that the commit triggered a run-through of the tests. Since we put the hook in the repository configuration file, it will only take effect on commits to this repository. If we'd instead put it into your personal configuration file, it would be called when you committed to any repository.

Bazaar

Like Git and Mercurial, Bazaar is a distributed version control system, and the individual users can control the hooks that apply to their own repositories. If you don't have Bazaar installed and don't plan to use it, you can skip this section.

Bazaar hooks go in your plugins directory. On Unix-like systems, that's `~/.bazaar/plugins/`, while on Windows, it's `C:\Documents and Settings\<username>\Application Data\Bazaar\<version>\plugins\`. In either case, you might have to create the plugins subdirectory, if it doesn't already exist.

Bazaar hooks are always written in Python, which is nice but, as I write this, they're always written in Python 2, not Python 3. This means that the hook code presented in this section is Python 2 code. Place the following code into a file called `run_nose.py` in the plugins directory:

```
from bzrlib import branch
from os.path import join, sep
from os import chdir
from subprocess import call

def run_nose(local, master, old_num, old_id, new_num, new_id):
    try:
        base = local.base
    except AttributeError:
        base = master.base

    if not base.startswith('file://'):
        return

    try:
        chdir(join(sep, *base[7:].split('/')))
    except OSError:
        return
```

```
        call(['nosetests'])

    branch.Branch.hooks.install_named_hook('post_commit',
                                           run_nose,
                                           'Runs Nose after each commit')
```

Bazaar hooks are written in Python, so we've written our hook as a function called `run_nose`. Our `run_nose` function checks in order to make sure that the repository we're working on is local, and then it changes directories into the repository and runs Nose. We registered `run_nose` as a hook by calling `branch.Branch.hooks.install_named_hook`.

From now on, any time you commit to a Bazaar repository, Nose will search for and run whatever tests it can find within that repository. Note that this applies to any and all local repositories, as long as you're logged in to the same account on your computer.

Automated continuous integration

Automated continuous integration tools are a step beyond using a version control hook to run your tests when you commit code to the repository. Instead of running your test suite once, an automated continuous integration system compiles your code (if need be) and runs your tests many times, in many different environments.

An automated continuous integration system might, for example, run your tests under Python versions 3.2, 3.3, and 3.4 on each of Windows, Linux, and Mac OS X. This not only lets you know about errors in your code, but also about the unexpected problems caused by the external environment. It's nice to know when that last patch broke the program on Windows, even though it worked like a charm on your Linux box.

Buildbot

Buildbot is a popular automated continuous integration tool. Using Buildbot, you can create a network of "build slaves" that will check your code each time you commit it to your repository. This network can be quite large, and it can be distributed around the Internet, so Buildbot works even for projects with lots of developers spread around the world.

Buildbot's home page is at `http://buildbot.net/`. By following links from this site, you can find the manual and download the latest version of the tool. At the time of writing, installing Buildbot with Python 3.x was slightly more complicated than just `pip install buildbot buildbot-slave`; thanks to some of the install files being targeted at Python 2.x. It's actually completely fine to install it with Python 2.x, and probably easier to deal with. Even if it's installed in Python 2.x, Buildbot can run your Python 3.x code inside the Python 3.x interpreter.

Buildbot operates in one of two modes, `buildmaster` and `buildslave`. A `buildmaster` mode manages a network of buildslaves, while the `buildslave` mode run the tests in their assorted environments.

Setup

To set up a `buildmaster` mode, create a directory for it to operate in and then run the following command:

```
$ buildbot create-master <directory>
```

In the preceding command, `<directory>` is the directory you just created for `buildbot` to work in.

Similarly, to set up a `buildslave` mode, create a directory for it to operate in and then run the command:

```
$ buildslave create-slave <directory> <host:port> <name> <password>
```

In the preceding command, `<directory>` is the directory you just created for the `buildbot` to work in, `<host:port>` is the Internet host and port where the `buildmaster` can be found, and `<name>` and `<password>` are the login information that identifies this `buildslave` to the `buildmaster`. All of this information (except the directory) is determined by the operator of the `buildmaster`.

You should edit `<directory>/info/admin` and `<directory>/info/host` to contain the e-mail address you want associated with this `buildslave` and a description of the `buildslave` operating environment, respectively.

On both the `buildmaster` and the `buildslave`, you'll need to start up the `buildbot` background process. To do this, use the command:

```
$ buildbot start <directory>
```

In the preceding command, the directory is the directory you set up as the `buildmaster`.

Configuring a `buildmaster` is a significant topic in itself, and one that we're not going to address in detail. It's fully described in Buildbot's own documentation. We will provide a simple configuration file, though, for reference and quick setup. This particular configuration file assumes that you're using Git, but it is not significantly different for other version control systems. The following code goes in the master's `<directory>/master.cfg` file:

```
# -*- python -*-
# ex: set syntax=python:
```

```
c = BuildmasterConfig = {}

c['projectName'] = "<replace with project name>"
c['projectURL'] = "<replace with project url>"
c['buildbotURL'] = "http://<replace with master url>:8010/"

c['status'] = []
from buildbot.status import html
c['status'].append(html.WebStatus(http_port=8010,
                                  allowForce=True))

c['slavePortnum'] = 9989

from buildbot.buildslave import BuildSlave
c['slaves'] = [
    BuildSlave("bot1name", "bot1passwd"),
    ]

from buildbot.changes.pb import PBChangeSource
c['change_source'] = PBChangeSource()

from buildbot.scheduler import Scheduler
c['schedulers'] = []
c['schedulers'].append(Scheduler(name="all", branch=None,
                                 treeStableTimer=2 * 60,
                                 builderNames=["buildbot-full"]))

from buildbot.process import factory
from buildbot.steps.source.git import Git
from buildbot.steps.shell import Test
f1 = factory.BuildFactory()
f1.addStep(Git(repourl="<replace with repository url>"))
f1.addStep(Test(command = ['python3', '-m' 'nose']))

b1 = {'name': "buildbot-full",
      'slavename': "bot1name",
      'builddir': "full",
      'factory': f1,
      }
c['builders'] = [b1]
```

We just set up Buildbot to run our tests whenever it notices that our source code has been unchanged for two hours.

We told it to run the tests by adding a build step that runs `nose`:

```
f1.addStep(Test(command = ['python3', '-m' 'nose']))
```

We told it to wait for the source code to be unchanged for two hours by adding a build scheduler:

```
c['schedulers'].append(Scheduler(name="all", branch=None,
                                 treeStableTimer=2 * 60,
                                 builderNames=["buildbot-full"]))
```

To make effective use of this Buildbot configuration, you also need to install a version control hook that notifies Buildbot of changes. Generically, this can be done by calling the `buildbot sendchange` shell command from the hook.

Once you have `buildmaster` and `buildslave` configured, have hooked `buildbot` into your version control system, and have started `buildmaster` and `buildslave`, you're in business.

Using Buildbot

You'll be able to see a report of the Buildbot status in your web browser, by navigating to the `buildbotURL` that you configured in the `master.cfg` file. One of the most useful reports is the so-called waterfall view. If the most recent commit passes the tests, you should see something similar to the following screenshot:

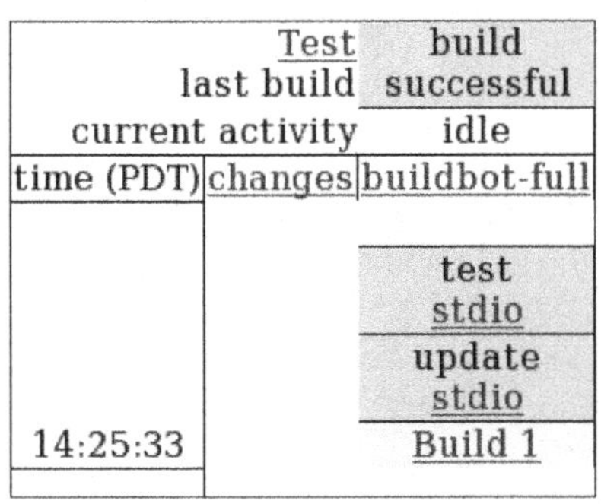

On the other hand, when the commit fails to pass the tests, you'll see the screenshot as follows:

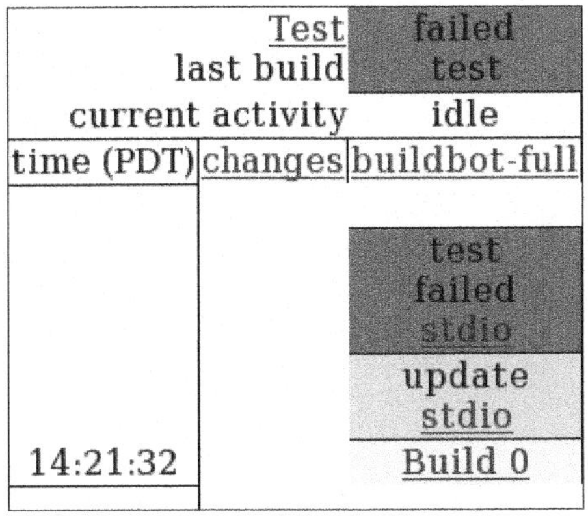

Either way, you'll also see a history of earlier versions, whether or not they passed the tests as well as who made the changes and when, and what the output of the test command looked like.

You'll see similar information for each of the buildslaves, which means that, when the tests pass on some systems and fail on others, you'll know which system configurations are having the problem.

Summary

We learned a lot in this chapter about code coverage and plugging our tests into the other automation systems we use while writing software.

Specifically, we covered what code coverage is and what it can tell us about our tests. We learned how to run Nose automatically when our version control software detects changes in the source code, and how to set up the Buildbot automated continuous integration system.

Now that we've learned about code coverage, version control hooks, and automated continuous integration, you're ready to tackle more or less anything. Congratulations!

Index

A

B

C

N

O

P

R

S

[PACKT] open source
community experience distilled
PUBLISHING

Thank you for buying
Learning Python Testing

About Packt Publishing

Packt, pronounced 'packed', published its first book "*Mastering phpMyAdmin for Effective MySQL Management*" in April 2004 and subsequently continued to specialize in publishing highly focused books on specific technologies and solutions.

Our books and publications share the experiences of your fellow IT professionals in adapting and customizing today's systems, applications, and frameworks. Our solution based books give you the knowledge and power to customize the software and technologies you're using to get the job done. Packt books are more specific and less general than the IT books you have seen in the past. Our unique business model allows us to bring you more focused information, giving you more of what you need to know, and less of what you don't.

Packt is a modern, yet unique publishing company, which focuses on producing quality, cutting-edge books for communities of developers, administrators, and newbies alike. For more information, please visit our website: `www.packtpub.com`.

About Packt Open Source

In 2010, Packt launched two new brands, Packt Open Source and Packt Enterprise, in order to continue its focus on specialization. This book is part of the Packt Open Source brand, home to books published on software built around Open Source licenses, and offering information to anybody from advanced developers to budding web designers. The Open Source brand also runs Packt's Open Source Royalty Scheme, by which Packt gives a royalty to each Open Source project about whose software a book is sold.

Writing for Packt

We welcome all inquiries from people who are interested in authoring. Book proposals should be sent to `author@packtpub.com`. If your book idea is still at an early stage and you would like to discuss it first before writing a formal book proposal, contact us; one of our commissioning editors will get in touch with you.

We're not just looking for published authors; if you have strong technical skills but no writing experience, our experienced editors can help you develop a writing career, or simply get some additional reward for your expertise.

CPSIA information can be obtained at www.ICGtesting.com
Printed in the USA
LVOW03s2226060115

421742LV00004B/198/P